| Abortion

Other Books of Related Interest:

At Issue Series
Do Abstinence Programs Work?
Foster Care
Is Parenthood a Right or a Privilege?
Reproductive Technologies
Should the Government Fund Embryonic Stem Cell Research?

Current Controversies Series
Human Genetics

Global Viewpoints Series
Population Growth

Introducing Issues with Opposing Viewpoints Series
Birth Control
China
Civil Liberties
Human Rights
Women's Rights

Issues on Trial
Abortion
Teen Parenting

Issues That Concern You
Teen Pregnancy

Opposing Viewpoints Series
Abortion
China
India

GLOBALVIEWPOINTS

Abortion

Noah Berlatsky, Book Editor

GREENHAVEN PRESS
A part of Gale, Cengage Learning

GALE
CENGAGE Learning·

Detroit • New York • San Francisco • New Haven, Conn • Waterville, Maine • London

c u p d

GALE
CENGAGE Learning·

Christine Nasso, *Publisher*
Elizabeth Des Chenes, *Managing Editor*

© 2011 Greenhaven Press, a part of Gale, Cengage Learning

Gale and Greenhaven Press are registered trademarks used herein under license.

For more information, contact:
Greenhaven Press
27500 Drake Rd.
Farmington Hills, MI 48331-3535
Or you can visit our Internet site at gale.cengage.com

For product information and technology assistance, contact us at

Gale Customer Support, 1-800-877-4253
For permission to use material from this text or product, submit all requests online at www.cengage.com/permissions

Further permissions questions can be emailed to permissionrequest@cengage.com

Articles in Greenhaven Press anthologies are often edited for length to meet page requirements. In addition, original titles of these works are changed to clearly present the main thesis and to explicitly indicate the author's opinion. Every effort is made to ensure that Greenhaven Press accurately reflects the original intent of the authors. Every effort has been made to trace the owners of copyrighted material.

Cover image © Staff/Reuters/Corbis.

LIBRARY OF CONGRESS CATALOGING-IN-PUBLICATION DATA

Abortion / Noah Berlatsky, book editor.
   p. cm. -- (Global viewpoints)
   Includes bibliographical references and index.
   ISBN 978-0-7377-4927-4 (hardcover) -- ISBN 978-0-7377-4928-1 (pbk.)
   1. Abortion--Juvenile literature. 2. Abortion--Religious aspects. I. Berlatsky, Noah.
   HQ767.2.A26 2010
   362.19'888--dc22

                                         2010005725

Printed in the United States of America
1 2 3 4 5 6 7 14 13 12 11 10

Contents

Chapter 1: Abortion and Religion

Jewish law on abortion does not fit easily into either pro-choice or pro-life philosophies. Judaism sees the fetus as a potential human being. Therefore, abortion is a very serious matter, though it may be permitted in certain situations.

Chapter 2: Abortion and the Law

Abortion is illegal in most circumstances in Jamaica. As a result, the poor in Jamaica have little access to safe, legal abortions. The legislature is considering changing the antiquated laws that contribute to this situation.

Chapter 3: Abortion and Sex Selection

In China, legal restrictions on the number of children, preference for male children, and technologies like ultrasound have caused many female fetuses to be aborted. There is scientific evidence that this has resulted in a gender imbalance. China is attempting to address this problem, and there is some evidence that the gender imbalance may soon decline.

Chapter 4: Abortion and Sex Education

A study found that peer-led sex education, in which students instructed each other, was not any more effective than teacher-led sex education in reducing abortion and teen pregnancy. Since teacher-led sex education is usually less time-consuming and controversial, the study suggests it may not be worth organizing peer-led programs.

Foreword

> *"The problems of all of humanity can only be solved by all of humanity."*
> —Swiss author Friedrich Dürrenmatt

Global interdependence has become an undeniable reality. Mass media and technology have increased worldwide access to information and created a society of global citizens. Understanding and navigating this global community is a challenge, requiring a high degree of information literacy and a new level of learning sophistication.

Building on the success of its flagship series, *Opposing Viewpoints*, Greenhaven Press has created the *Global Viewpoints* series to examine a broad range of current, often controversial topics of worldwide importance from a variety of international perspectives. Providing students and other readers with the information they need to explore global connections and think critically about worldwide implications, each *Global Viewpoints* volume offers a panoramic view of a topic of widespread significance.

Drugs, famine, immigration—a broad, international treatment is essential to do justice to social, environmental, health, and political issues such as these. Junior high, high school, and early college students, as well as general readers, can all use *Global Viewpoints* anthologies to discern the complexities relating to each issue. Readers will be able to examine unique national perspectives while, at the same time, appreciating the interconnectedness that global priorities bring to all nations and cultures.

Material in each volume is selected from a diverse range of sources, including journals, magazines, newspapers, nonfiction books, speeches, government documents, pamphlets, organization newsletters, and position papers. *Global Viewpoints* is truly global, with material drawn primarily from international sources available in English and secondarily from U.S. sources with extensive international coverage.

Features of each volume in the *Global Viewpoints* series include:

- An **annotated table of contents** that provides a brief summary of each essay in the volume, including the name of the country or area covered in the essay.

- An **introduction** specific to the volume topic.

- A **world map** to help readers locate the countries or areas covered in the essays.

- For each viewpoint, an **introduction** that contains notes about the author and source of the viewpoint explains why material from the specific country is being presented, summarizes the main points of the viewpoint, and offers three **guided reading questions** to aid in understanding and comprehension.

- **For further discussion** questions that promote critical thinking by asking the reader to compare and contrast aspects of the viewpoints or draw conclusions about perspectives and arguments.

- A worldwide list of **organizations to contact** for readers seeking additional information.

- A **periodical bibliography** for each chapter and a **bibliography of books** on the volume topic to aid in further research.

- A comprehensive **subject index** to offer access to people, places, events, and subjects cited in the text, with the countries covered in the viewpoints highlighted.

Global Viewpoints is designed for a broad spectrum of readers who want to learn more about current events, history, political science, government, international relations, economics, environmental science, world cultures, and sociology—students doing research for class assignments or debates, teachers and faculty seeking to supplement course materials, and others wanting to understand current issues better. By presenting how people in various countries perceive the root causes, current consequences, and proposed solutions to worldwide challenges, *Global Viewpoints* volumes offer readers opportunities to enhance their global awareness and their knowledge of cultures worldwide.

Introduction

"With the passing of the bill, Nicaragua became one of just three countries in the Western Hemisphere to ban medical abortions, even when a pregnant woman's life was at risk or she had been the victim of rape or incest."

—Kate Seelye,
*"The Cost of Nicaragua's
Total Abortion Ban,"*
FRONTLINE/World,
March 13, 2008

Abortion, or the medical termination of pregnancy, is an extremely controversial issue in all parts of the world. One particularly intense argument surrounding abortion has occurred in the Central American nation of Nicaragua. Between 55–70 percent of Nicaraguans are Catholic, with many of the rest belonging to conservative evangelical churches, according to a 2009 U.S. State Department report on international religious freedom. Public opinion tends to support the Catholic Church's strong opposition to abortion. Thus, Nicaraguan abortion law has long been restrictive. Under laws in effect since the 1890s, abortions were illegal in most cases. A person who performed an abortion was subject to three to six years in prison; and if a woman consented to an abortion, she could be subject to a prison term of one to four years, according to the 2002 United Nations (UN) report, *Abortion Policies: A Global Review*. However, the law did allow "therapeutic abortion," which was not strictly defined, but appeared to cover situations where the continuation of the pregnancy would result in the death of the mother. To undergo a therapeutic abortion, the law stated, a woman had to obtain the recommendation of three physicians and the consent of her husband or her closest relative.

According to the UN report, "In the mid-1980s, 45 percent of all admissions to the largest maternity hospital at Managua were the result of illegal abortion." Because of figures like this, medical professionals and health organizations advocated to liberalize abortion laws. These efforts received additional impetus from a high-profile 2003 case involving a nine-year-old girl publicly called "Rosita." Rosita was pregnant due to a rape, and her parents were determined to obtain an abortion for her. Government officials attempted to have her removed from her parents to prevent the termination of the pregnancy, but eventually with the help of women's advocacy groups, she did obtain an abortion.

At that point, "Nicaragua's archbishop excommunicat[ed] everyone connected to the abortion," according to the Web site of Attie&Goldwater Productions, which produced a documentary film about Rosita and the controversy surrounding her pregnancy. The archbishop argued that no action was needed on his part; those involved in the abortion had simply excommunicated themselves. In either case, the archbishop's statements on the matter led "tens of thousands of women in Nicaragua—and supporters in Europe—to sign petitions demanding to be excommunicated," according to a 2003 report by Sue Chan on the CBS News Web site. The incident also touched off a furious nationwide debate, in which Nicaragua's health minister Lucia Salvo, who had been against the abortion, was forced to resign and the country's restrictive abortion laws were publicly questioned.

Despite this incident, however, Nicaragua's abortion laws did not become less restrictive. Instead, in 2006, the legislature passed a law eliminating the exception for therapeutic pregnancies in cases where the woman's life was threatened. The law was passed right before national elections, and was supported by both parties in what a *New York Times* editorial called "a clear bid to curry support from the Catholic Church."

Orlando Tardencilla, one of the legislators who proposed the bill, was quoted in an October 26, 2006, article on the BBC News Web site arguing for the ban. "Unless abortion is made a crime," Tardencilla maintained, "then people can simply come out and say: 'I have the right to an abortion, this is my body and I can decide.' That's like saying: 'I'm allowed to commit murder because these hands are mine, this gun is mine.'"

The BBC News story noted that the more restrictive law appeared to have public support. However, a poll reported by the Angus Reid Global Monitor on December 4, 2006, suggested that public opinion was not in favor of the change. In the poll, 69 percent agreed that abortions in cases where the woman's life was threatened should be legal, while only 28 percent felt that abortions should be illegal in such cases.

The organization Human Rights Watch came out strongly against the ban in an October 2007 report by Marianne Mollmann titled *Over Their Dead Bodies*. The report states that preventing women from receiving abortions in cases where their lives are in danger "directly contravenes international human rights standards on the right to life, the right to health, the right to nondiscrimination, and a number of other established human rights." The report argues that women in Nicaragua will seek out dangerous illegal abortions, and that, out of fear of prosecution, doctors may even deny emergency obstetric care that does not involve abortion. In the report a doctor at a public hospital in Managua is quoted describing a woman who "needed a therapeutic abortion," but, because of the law, was left without treatment. The fetus was born dead, and the women "was already in septic shock and died five days later."

A 2009 report by Amnesty International similarly argued that the ban "is endangering the lives of girls and women, denying them lifesaving treatment, preventing health professionals from practicing effective medicine and contributing to an increase in maternal deaths."

However, proponents of the ban deny that there has been an increase in maternal deaths. Father Thomas Euteneuer of the pro-life group Human Life International, for example, dismissed such accusations in a 2007 article reprinted on the Web site Big Blue Wave. Euteneuer noted that according to the Nicaraguan health minister, maternal deaths had actually fallen by one in the year following the elimination of therapeutic abortions. According to Euteneuer, most of these deaths were due to "hypertension, drugs, violence, inability to access health services and other health concerns not related to the ban on abortion."

Very few countries have a ban as extreme as Nicaragua's, yet most countries, to one extent or another, face the issues raised by Nicaragua's abortion policy. The following viewpoints look at these issues in chapters that include Abortion and Religion, Abortion and the Law, Abortion and Sex Selection, and Abortion and Sex Education. Such discussions show that—from Japan to Ireland, from Jamaica to Australia—human rights organizations, religious groups, and individuals continue to debate the moral and legal status of abortion.

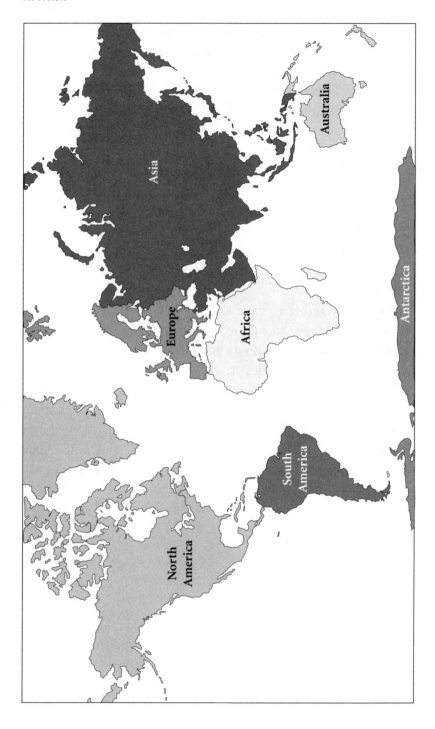

CHAPTER 1

Abortion and Religion

Buddhism Opposes but Does Not Condemn Abortion

Damien Keown

Damien Keown is a bioethicist specializing in Buddhist ethics at the University of London. In the following viewpoint, he explains that Buddhism traditionally condemns the taking of any human life and has therefore seen abortion as wrong. However, Buddhists treat moral lapses with compassion rather than condemnation. As a result, there is little Buddhist activism against abortion in Buddhist nations like Thailand and Japan.

As you read, consider the following questions:

1. What is the first precept of Buddhism, and how does it influence the discussion of abortion?
2. According to this viewpoint, what are the five aggregates or *skandhas*?
3. According to Keown, why has the issue of abortion been particularly acute in Japan?

How do Buddhist ethical teachings like *ahimsā* [the Buddhist precept that one should do no harm] affect its approach to abortion? Is Buddhism 'pro-life' or 'pro-choice'? The Buddhist belief in rebirth clearly introduces a new dimension to the abortion debate. For one thing, it puts the question

'When does life begin?'—a key question in the context of abortion—in an entirely new light. For Buddhism, life is a continuum with no discernible starting point, and birth and death are like a revolving door through which an individual passes again and again.

But does belief in rebirth increase or reduce the seriousness of abortion? It may be thought that it reduces it, since all that has been done is to postpone rebirth to a later time—the child that was to have been born simply arrives later. Traditional sources, however, do not take this view, and regard the intentional killing of a human being at any stage of life as wrong, regardless of the fact that he or she will be born again. . . .

Abortion Violates Buddhist Precepts

Interpreting the traditional teachings in the light of modern scientific discoveries such as ovulation, the most common view among Buddhists today, particularly those from traditional countries, is that fertilization is the point at which individual human life commences. As a consequence, abortion is widely seen as contrary to the first precept. As already noted, the precept prohibits causing harm to anything which has *pāna* . . . which means both 'life' and 'breath'. Because of the reference to 'breath' here, it could be argued that since a fetus does not breathe, it does not fall within the scope of the precept. The sense of the term *pāna*, however, is not restricted to respiration and rather connotes the idea of 'vital breath' or the 'breath of life'. In medical contexts *pāna* is one of the bodily humours, understood as the force underlying biological growth, perhaps equivalent to the contemporary notion of metabolism. Since this process occurs throughout all stages of fetal life, it is difficult to argue that the moral protection of the first precept does not apply to the unborn. Moreover, since this metabolic process continues throughout gestation (and beyond), it is difficult to ground arguments that seek to draw a line at a certain stage of fetal development—such as viability, which occurs around the 24th week—in order to establish a point up to which abortion may be allowed.

Any ambiguity there may be thought to be in the first precept with respect to abortion is removed in the equivalent precept in the Vinaya [Buddhist teachings based on canonical texts orally passed down by the Buddha] . . . which prohibits taking a human life. . . . One formulation of the precept . . . explicitly mentions abortion, and the commentary explains that the prohibition applies from the moment of conception. Although strictly speaking this precept applies only to monks and nuns, it confirms that life was thought to begin at conception rather than some later point.

The early teachings are consistent in depicting abortion as an immoral act that brings karmic suffering in its wake.

Despite the condemnation of abortion, the case histories recorded in the Vinaya disclose that as medical practitioners monks occasionally became illegally involved in procuring and performing abortions. Monks frequently acted as counsellors to families, and often were drawn into the kinds of problems that arise in family life, such as an unwanted pregnancy. The motives reported in the sources for seeking an abortion include concealing extramarital affairs, as when a married woman becomes pregnant by her lover, seeking to prevent an inheritance by aborting the rightful heir prior to birth, and domestic rivalry between co-wives due to the pregnancy of one affecting the position and status of another. Sometimes monks brought their medical knowledge to bear in an attempt to cause a miscarriage. The methods used included ointments, potions, and charms, pressing or crushing the womb, and scorching or heating it. Monks who were involved in performing or procuring abortions were expelled from the *sangha* [the monkish community] for life, the severest sanction available.

Other more popular literature describes the evil karmic consequences of abortion, sometimes in lurid detail. Stories ... narrate the evil consequences which follow an abortion, such as the loss of offspring in future lives, acts of revenge, and rebirth in hell. At both a popular and scholarly level, therefore, the early teachings are consistent in depicting abortion as an immoral act that brings karmic suffering in its wake.

Human Beings and Persons

Much of the philosophical discussion of abortion in the West has focused on the criteria of moral personhood and the point at which a fetus acquires the capacities that entitle it to moral respect. The philosophical foundations for this approach were laid by [British philosopher John] Locke and [German philosopher Immanuel] Kant, who argued that only rational beings are 'persons' with moral status. For them, the paradigm moral subject is the adult in possession of all his or her intellectual faculties. Locke and Kant did not apply these conclusions to abortion, but building on their views contemporary philosophers who take a liberal position on abortion argue that what we value about human beings is not life *per se*, in the biological sense, but rather the various faculties and powers human beings possess, such as reason, self-consciousness, autonomy, the capacity to form relationships, and similar abilities of this kind. When these faculties are present, they say, we can speak of a moral 'person', and when they are absent there is only biological life. On this reasoning, before it acquires these attributes, a fetus is only a 'potential person' rather than an actual one, and so does not have a claim to full moral status and the right to life that entails.

As an example of this approach, contemporary feminist writers such as Mary Anne Warren have identified five features central to personhood—consciousness, reasoning, self-motivated activity, the capacity to communicate, and self-awareness. Warren claims that a fetus is no more conscious or rational than a fish, and that accordingly abortion is not immoral. Opponents have responded by pointing to the vagueness and arbitrariness of the criteria suggested (for instance, are the movements of a fetus in the womb, such as kicking, a form of 'communication' with its mother?) and the difficulty of determining when and to what degree faculties such as reasoning are present. Conservative opponents use 'slippery slope' arguments against the liberal position, claiming that a secure line cannot be drawn at any one point in the development of the fetus. They suggest that such lines are vague and can usually be pushed back down the slope of fetal development towards conception as the only clear point of origin for individual human life.

Persons and *Skandhas*

A Buddhist pro-choice argument paralleling that based on the concept of personhood could be mounted by reference to the doctrine of the five aggregates (*skandhas*). These are the five factors that constitute the individual human being, [material form, feelings and sensations, perceptions, volitions, and consciousness]. . . .

If it could be shown, for instance, that these five endowments were acquired gradually rather than all at once, it may be possible to argue that the life of an early fetus which possessed fewer of the five was less valuable than that of a more mature one, which possessed them all. The second aggregate relating to the faculty of feeling, for instance, may be thought of as absent or not well developed in an embryo or very young fetus, since the capacity to feel depends on the development of a brain and central nervous system. This argument faces the problem that according to the early commentarial tradition all five *skandhas* are present from the moment of rebirth (in other words, from conception). Buddhaghosa [an Indian Buddhist scholar of the fifth century], for instance, is very clear in stating that the human mind–body aggregate . . . is complete in the very first moment of existence as a human being. This means that the body . . . and the other four aggregates of feelings . . . , conceptions . . . , mental formations . . . , and consciousness . . . form a unity from the outset rather than developing gradually as the fetus evolves.

The doctrine of rebirth, moreover, sees the new conceptus as not just a 'potential person' evolving for the first time from nothing, but as a continuing entity bearing the complete karmic encoding of a recently deceased individual. [Karma is the concept of actions resulting in spiritual consequences—the actions of a past life will affect the conditions of future lives.] If we rewind the karmic tape a short way, perhaps just a few hours, to the point when death occurred in the previous life, we would typically find an adult man or woman fulfilling all the requirements of 'personhood'. The bodily form at rebirth has changed, but the bodily form of human beings changes constantly, and according to Buddhist teachings we have before us at conception the same individual only now at an immature state of physical development. Given the continuity of the human subject through thousands of lifetimes, it seems arbitrary to apply labels such as 'actual' or 'potential' to any given stage and to claim that the individual repeatedly gains and then loses the moral protection of the first precept.

It is sometimes suggested that Buddhism regards late abortions as morally worse than earlier ones. This view is based on a remark of Buddhaghosa in his commentary on the Vinaya . . . to the effect that the size of the victim is one of two important criteria (the other being sanctity) in assessing the gravity of breaches of the first precept. Since a fetus is considerably larger at the end of its term, it has been argued that late abortions are worse than earlier ones. This line of argument, however, fails to appreciate that Buddhaghosa's comments with respect to size were made purely with reference to animals. Thus, . . . it is worse to kill a large animal, such as an elephant, than a mouse, because it involves a greater degree of effort and determination, and the will to cause harm on the part of the assailant is greater. Clearly, the criterion of size is not meant to be applied in the case of human beings, otherwise it would lead to the ludicrous conclusion that killing large people was worse than killing small people. The argument that early abortions are morally less serious because the fetus is smaller, therefore, is based upon a misunderstanding of Buddhaghosa's criterion.

The doctrine of rebirth . . . sees the new conceptus as not just a "potential person" evolving for the first time from nothing, but as a continuing entity bearing the complete karmic encoding of a recently deceased individual.

Abortion in Thailand

Turning now to the contemporary situation, things are much less tidy and consistent than they appear in the classical sources. There is considerable variation across the Buddhist world, much divergence between theory and practice, and a fair amount of what might be called 'moral dissonance', whereby individuals experience themselves as pulled in contradictory directions.

Given the attitude to abortion in the classical scriptures, in the more traditional Buddhist countries such as Sri Lanka and Thailand, abortion is illegal with certain limited exceptions, such as when necessary to save the mother's life or in the case of rape. The relevant Thai law is the Penal Code of 1956, which imposes strict penalties: A woman who causes an abortion for herself or procures one from someone else can expect to face a penalty of three years in prison and a fine of 3,000 baht [about 90 dollars], or both. The penalty for the abortionist is even greater: five years or 5,000 baht [about 150 dollars], or both, and if the woman is injured or killed in the process the penalties are much more severe. Official statistics from the 1960s report some five abortions per year, but this massively underestimates the number of abortions performed. This is because illegal abortions are very common with perhaps 300,000 such procedures a year in Thailand performed in the many hundreds of illegal abortion clinics found throughout the country but particularly in rural areas. This figure is equivalent to 37 abortions per 1,000 women of childbearing age. By way of comparison, some statistics from other countries are: Canada, 11.1; USA, 24.2; Hungary; 35.3; Japan, 22.6 (officially, but probably between 65 and 90); Singapore, 44.5; in the former USSR [Soviet Union] the figure was an astonishing 181. According to a 1987 study, the majority of abortions (around 80–90%) in Thailand were performed for married woman, mostly agricultural workers. The study also confirmed that abortion was the accepted method of birth control among these women, suggesting that if better contraception was available the number of abortions would drop sharply.

One interesting aspect of the Thai situation is the low profile maintained by Buddhist monks, who rarely comment or become involved on one side or the other of the [abortion] argument.

Despite the basic religious objection to abortion, Thai attitudes towards the issue are complex and researchers often encounter contradictory positions. A 1998 survey mainly of medical staff in Thailand revealed ambivalent attitudes, with most respondents reporting negative feelings after the procedure, including 36% who were concerned about the bad karma likely to result from it. While nearly all medical staff supported abortions for women who had been raped, who were HIV positive, or who had contracted German measles in the first trimester of pregnancy, 70% were opposed to abortion on socioeconomic grounds. Similarly, while a very high proportion of those surveyed viewed abortion as a threat to Thai values, 55% of the medical staff favoured a liberalization of Thai abortion laws.

One interesting aspect of the Thai situation is the low profile maintained by Buddhist monks, who rarely comment or become involved on one side or the other of the argument. With rare exceptions, monks do not picket abortion clinics, go on protest marches, or counsel women who are considering having an abortion, as clergy or activists in the West might do. This is not because they have no position on the matter, and if pressed almost all would agree that abortion is immoral. For the most part, however, they prefer to regard it as a secular or 'village' matter in which they have no direct involvement, and seem content to leave the decision to the conscience of the individuals involved. To a large extent, this apparent aloofness has to do with matters of decorum and the high status in which the monkhood is held. Most Buddhist lay folk, and particularly women, would feel embarrassment at discussing such intimate matters with monks, and prefer to discuss the problem with a doctor or other secular professional. Many monks, too, feel that these questions are not proper for one who has renounced the world and is pursuing the spiritual life. This attitude is changing, although slowly.

Abortion in Japan

Elsewhere in Asia, attitudes and practices relating to abortion vary quite widely. In Japan (where Buddhism has been influential but is not the state religion), abortion is legal and around a million abortions are performed each year. This compares with a figure of 1.3 million for the United States, a country with over twice the population of Japan. (The annual total for the United Kingdom is around 180,000).

What many see as a constructive contribution to the dilemma posed by abortion has been developed in recent decades by Japanese Buddhists. The issue of abortion has been particularly acute in Japan because the contraceptive pill has not been widely available, apparently because of concerns about possible side effects. In the absence of effective prevention, an efficient (and profitable) abortion industry has emerged to deal with the problem of unwanted pregnancies. Faced with the anguish these situations create, Japanese society has searched its ancient cultural heritage and evolved a unique solution, in the form of the *mizuko kuyō* memorial service for aborted children. Only ever resorted to by a minority of women who had abortions or miscarriages, the ritual became extremely popular in the 1960s and 1970s, although it is now less common.

'*Mizuko*' literally means 'water child', a concept that has its origins in Japanese mythology, and '*kuyō*' means a ritual or ceremony. The *mizuko kuyō* service is generally a simple one in which a small figure of the bodhisattva Jizō represents the departed child. Jizō Bosatsu is a popular bodhisattva [an enlightened being who is worthy of nirvana, or heaven, but postpones it in order to help others] in Japan who is regarded as the protector of young children, and statues and shrines to him are found throughout the country. He is often shown dressed in the robes of a monk carrying a staff with six rings on it, which jingle like a child's rattle. The rings represent the six realms of rebirth in traditional Buddhist teachings, and Jizō visits each of these realms to help those in need. Jizō's origins lie in India as the bodhisattva Ksitigarbha ('womb of the earth'), but when his cult reached Japan he became associated with a folk-belief concerning the fate of children who die young, known as *mizuko* or 'water babies'. Such children were thought to go to an underworld or realm of the shades, a limbo in which they awaited rebirth. In the popular imagination, this place was identified with a deserted river bank called

Sai-no-kawara in Meido. There, they seek to amuse themselves by day playing with pebbles on the beach, but when night comes they become cold and afraid, and it is then that Jizō comes to enfold them in his robe and cheer them with the jingling sound of his staff. This scene is often depicted in statues and described in hymns. . . .

The public nature of the ceremonial simultaneously acknowledges the child that has been lost and helps those involved come to terms with the event on an emotional level. Women who have the ritual performed find it consoling, and it is clearly comforting to think that Jizō is protecting their lost offspring. . . .

Japan has not seen the kinds of attacks on abortion clinics and their personnel that have taken place in the USA. This approach is in line with the nonjudgmental stance Buddhism traditionally adopts on moral issues.

Opposition to Abortion in Japan

The ritual, however, is not without its critics. The majority of Buddhist organizations in Japan do not endorse *mizuko kuyō*, regarding it as a modern innovation based on questionable theology. . . . One of the largest Buddhist organizations in Japan, the Jōdō Shinshū, actively opposes the rite for this reason, pointing out that according to orthodox Buddhist teachings a ritual cannot wipe away the bad karma caused by an abortion. The more unscrupulous temples in Japan have also sometimes exploited the ritual commercially, promoting the idea of *tatari*, or retribution from departed spirits. The idea has been put about, often accompanied by lurid pictures, that an aborted fetus becomes a vengeful spirit that causes problems for the mother unless placated by the ritual. Undoubtedly, many temples saw the ritual simply as a money-making scheme and ruthlessly exploited vulnerable women.

Opposition on the part of the Jōdō Shinshū and others, however, has not taken a political form, and Japanese Buddhists have not campaigned to change the law on abortion or sought to influence the practice of the medical profession. Japan has not seen the kinds of attacks on abortion clinics and their personnel that have taken place in the USA. This approach is in line with the nonjudgmental stance Buddhism traditionally adopts on moral issues. It recognizes that the pressures and complexities of daily life can cloud the judgment and lead people to make wrong choices. The appropriate response in these cases, however, is thought to be compassion and understanding rather than vociferous condemnation.

Pro-Choice in Buddhism

Early scriptural sources oppose abortion, regarding it as a breach of the first precept, a view generally followed in traditional countries despite the evidence that large numbers of 'backstreet' abortions are carried out. Some contemporary Buddhists, especially in the West, however, feel that there is more to be said on the morality of abortion than is found in the ancient sources, and that there may be circumstances in which abortion may be justified. For one thing, early Buddhist attitudes were formulated in a society that took a very different view of the status of women from that of the modern West. Feminist writers have drawn attention to the patriarchal nature of traditional societies and to the institutionalized repression of women down the centuries (other scholars deny that either of these historical claims is correct, except at specific times and places). It has also been argued that abortion rights are integral to the emancipation of women and are necessary to redress injustice. Buddhists who are sympathetic to this view and who support the notion of the woman's 'right to choose' may recommend meditation and discussion with a Buddhist teacher as ways in which the woman can get in touch with her feelings and come to a decision in harmony with her conscience. As the encounter between Buddhism and

31

Western values proceeds, discussions over the abortion question are certain to continue, hopefully producing more light and less heat than has been the tendency in the past.

Hindu Ethics About Abortion Are Very Different from Western Ones

Edward Omar Moad

Edward Omar Moad is a postdoctoral fellow at the Department of Philosophy at the National University of Singapore. In the following viewpoint, he argues that Hindu attitudes toward abortion are influenced by the belief in reincarnation and the mingling of social and moral concerns. In general, Hinduism opposes abortion except to save the life of the mother, but the reasoning behind this position is very different from that in the pro-life/ pro-choice debate in the West. Thus, the Hindu position on abortion is neither based in an idea of universal rights nor in social good, but on ideas about reincarnation, caste, and dharma, or righteous duty.

As you read, consider the following questions:

1. According to Moad, what rights are often balanced against each other in Western discussions of abortion?

2. For Hindus, why is the time in the womb painful, torturous, and repulsive?

Edward Omar Moad, "Hindu Ethics on the Moral Question of Abortion," *Eubios Journal of Asian and International Bioethics*, vol. 14, 2004, pp. 149–150. Reproduced by permission.

3. According to Moad, what is the worst punishment that could be inflicted upon a member of traditional Hindu society?

In the West, especially in the United States, the debate over the issue of abortion is one of the most controversial subjects of the day. The arguments employed by each side commonly originate from theological sources on the one hand, and scientific sources on the other. Part of the reason for the position of this controversy, among others, in the Western public consciousness is that it has implications affecting the moral value of human life, the source of that value, and the question over when a human being can be said to acquire this value. Thus, the argument usually ends up turning around whether life begins at conception, at birth, or at some point in between. There are arguments over the difference between living beings in general and persons, what constitutes personhood as an entitlement to rights, and so on. Taking a look at the issue from a global perspective, it becomes apparent that the ways in which these debates develop are fundamentally shaped by the cultural context in which they are held.

In the United States, for example, the argument is almost always centered on the Western concept of inalienable rights. It is the "rights of the unborn" against the "rights of women". Fathers and grandparents are often eager to assert their rights as well. Dealing with social issues like abortion on a cross-cultural level requires one to temporarily transcend, as much as possible, the cultural context within which one is immersed. Failure to do so can be the cause of a number of blunders, the most common of which, in connection with our topic, is the quixotic and uneducated reactions that are frequently expressed toward, for example, China's one-child policy [China has legally restricted couples to one child]. The purpose of this [viewpoint] will be to ascertain the traditional view of abortion in India, and explore, as much as possible, the context of religious and ethical values and rationale behind it.

The Soul of the Fetus in Hinduism

Perhaps the best place to begin would be at that most important question in the Western abortion debate: When does the life of a human being become sacred? Or to put it in metaphysical terms, when does the fetus receive a soul? This way, an important difference in the Hindu cultural context surrounding the issue will become clear; specifically, that such a question is almost irrelevant. Nevertheless, it is not an unanswered one.

The Hindu view of a person is a central theme of the Hindu scriptures. Basically, it is a dualistic model consisting of *atman* (roughly, spirit), and *prakrti* (matter). According to the *Caraka Samhita*, a Hindu medical text, the soul is already joined with matter in the act of conception. The soul is described as descending "... into the union of semen and (menstrual) blood in the womb in keeping with the (karmically produced) psychic disposition (of the embryonic matter)." Though there are a few differing traditions on this matter (the *Garbha Upanishad* [one of the core Hindu scriptures] claims that ensoulment takes place in the seventh month), they are considered to be based on weaker evidence, and the mainstream of Hindu thought coincides with this position. Thus, the traditional Hindu view of the time of ensoulment is similar to that expressed by Thomas Aquinas [a medieval Catholic theologian], for example. However, there are important differences in other aspects. The *Vishnu Purana* [an important Hindu religious text] describes consciousness in the womb:

"An individual soul (*jantu*), possessing a subtle body (*sukumaratanu*), resides in his mother's womb (*garbha*), which is imbued with various sorts of impurity (*mala*). He stays there being folded in the membrane surrounding the foetus [fetus] (*ulba*). . . . He experiences severe pains . . . tormented immensely by the foods his mother takes . . . incapable of extending (*prasarana*) or contracting (*akuncana*) his own limbs and reposing amidst a mud of faeces [feces] and urine, he is in every way incommoded. He is unable to breathe. Yet, being endowed with consciousness (*sacaitanya*) and thus calling to memory many hundreds (of previous) births, he resides in his mother's womb with great pains, being bound by his previous deeds."

According to the Caraka Samhita, *a Hindu medical text, the soul is already joined with matter in the act of conception.*

Reincarnation and Opposition to Abortion

The obvious difference between this Hindu description of life in the womb and that perceived in the West arises from the concept of reincarnation. The soul in the womb is not a new soul. Rather it contemplates its previous births. Thus, the hiatus in the womb is not seen in nearly as positive a light as it is in Western thought. It is painful, torturous, and repulsive; the evil result of attachment to physical existence displayed in one's past lives. In the Hindu context, the purpose of life as a human being is to make progress toward liberation from rebirth. The most important thing for each soul is the unfolding of its karmic destiny toward this goal. Abortion can obstruct this unfolding, and therefore it is condemned, but for vastly different reasons than it is in the West.

The practice of abortion is negatively referred to in the earliest Hindu scriptures, the Vedas. These texts comprise the *sruti*, those scriptures considered to have primary authority in Hindu thought. In the *Rg Samhit*, possibly originating from before 1200 BC, Vishnu [a major Hindu god] is called "protector of the child-to-be", implying that the fetus was deserving of even divine reverence. Meanwhile, the *Atharva Veda* expresses the following explicit pleas regarding those who perform abortions:

"With what bonds the overslaughed [passed over] one is bound apart, applied and tied up on each limb—let them be released, for they are releasers; wipe off difficulties, O Pushan, on the embryo slayer."

"Enter thou after the beams, the smokes, O evil; go unto the mists or also the fogs; disappear along those foams of the rivers: wipe off difficulties, O Pushan, on the embryo slayer."

Evidently, the "embryo slayer" is seen as a suitable candidate to bear the sufferings and sins of the rest of the Vedic community. The *Satapatha Brahmana* compares the reputation of those who eat beef with those who perform abortions, while in the Upanisads they are placed in a category with thieves and outcastes.

In the Hindu context, the purpose of life as a human being is to make progress toward liberation from rebirth. . . . Abortion can obstruct this unfolding, and therefore it is condemned, but for vastly different reasons than it is in the West.

The later *smrti* texts also contain injunctions against abortion, as well as protections for pregnant women. In the *Visnudharmasutra* [a source of Indian law], killing either fetus or mother is equated to the worst crime possible in Hindu society, killing a Brahmin [a member of the highest caste, such as priests]. Ferrymen and toll collectors are prescribed punishment for collection from pregnant women. The *Mahabharata*, [an important Indian epic] likewise, lists expectant mothers among a group that one must "give way to" that includes Brahmin, cows, and kings.

The worst penalty that could be inflicted upon a member of traditional Hindu society was to lose one's caste. [In India, caste is the station and occupation into which an individual is born.] This effectively removed one from the social structure altogether, and even had tragic implications on one's pros-

---

Hinduism on Abortion

It is important to note here that the karmic repercussions of abortion, grave though they may be, are not "punishments" in the sense of being the personal vengeance of a wrathful, judgmental God. They are simply the consequences of violating a natural law—whether that law is violated out of ignorance, fear, or whatever other possible motive. [Hindu] spiritual leaders are . . . intending . . . to help people become more mindful and compassionate in their behavior, and to promote the evolution of all the souls that may be harmed through an abortion—the child's, the mother's, the father's, the abortion provider's.

Parsuram Maharaj,
Trinidad and Tobago's Newsday,
July 6, 2004. http://newsday.co.tt.

Two crimes that call for a woman to have her caste re-voked are sexual relations with a man of lower caste and abortion.

---

pects for spiritual liberation. The *Gautamadharmasutra* [a source of Indian law] tells us that two crimes that call for a woman to have her caste revoked are sexual relations with a man of lower caste and abortion. Though the abortion of the fetus of a Brahmin is punishable by more extreme penalties than that of a slave, even those who perform abortions on slaves were fined. This difference in treatment reflects the belief that Brahmins were at a stage closer to spiritual liberation, and thus the uniquely Hindu rationale against abortion.

Moral, Not Social

Hindu ideology made an exception however, when abortion became necessary to save the life of the mother. The *Susruta Samhita*, another Hindu medical text, describes a procedure to induce birth during complications in the pregnancy. The ultimate objective is, of course, saving the mother and the baby. However, in the event that this is not a possibility, the text affirms, saving the mother takes precedence, and an abortion is justified.

Hindu ideology made an exception . . . when abortion became necessary to save the life of the mother.

This serves as evidence against the possible assertion that the real basis for an anti-abortion attitude in Hindu society stems solely from social goals related to supplying sons for the family and the caste. If that were true, and the moral sentiment played no role, then surely the mother would be considered less important than the child. Such a charge, furthermore, could be another example of the mistake of superimposing categories that are relevant within the context of one culture, onto an issue in another culture, where they are meaningless. The concept of Hindu dharma [one's righteous duty], the basis of ethics in Hindu society, makes no distinction between social and moral motivations. In fact, the two are inextricably enmeshed in each other. Thus, as much as it would be false to say that to bear sons is not highly valued among Hindus, it is equally false to discard the expression of moral rationale against abortion as artificial. Besides the fact that all the Sanskrit words for abortion have highly negative connotations related to killing, such as *hatya* [which means "murder"], the way in which abortion is dealt with in relation to the rigors of the caste system strongly suggest a primacy of moral over social concerns.

As I have noted above, the two crimes for which a woman could lose her caste were sex with a lower caste male and abortion. In cases where there had been a sexual relationship between a higher caste female and a lower caste male that resulted in offspring, it posed a complicated problem for the Hindu society. Such children could not be accepted into any caste and therefore constituted various categories of "outcastes", classless populations with no position in society that ushered in all the myriad social problems associated with such situations. Outcastes had everything going against them, and were generally destined for a miserable life. Despite this fact, abortion was never allowed as an acceptable solution. The lives of these fetuses, with all the social consequences that were involved in their births, were believed to have a moral status that protected them from early termination.

Hopefully, this [viewpoint] has scratched the surface of Hindu thought relating to abortion enough to make it clear that in India (despite not being nearly as public as it is in the West) it is an issue unique to Hindu ethical thought. It does not involve the ultimate value of the embodiment of the soul, as expressed by traditional Western religious viewpoints. Nor can it be reduced to a utilitarian equation aimed at the benefit of society as a whole or a particular class, as the various Western liberal and secular interpretations would have it. It is a question, which, for Hindus, may be dealt with only on uniquely Hindu terms.

Islam Condemns Almost All Abortions After Four Months

Muhammad ibn Adam al-Kawthari

Muhammad ibn Adam al-Kawthari is an Islamic scholar who teaches at Darul Uloom Leicester, an institution of higher Islamic learning in Britain. In the following viewpoint, he explains that Islam considers life sacred. For this reason, abortion is a very serious matter. According to al-Kawthari, the soul in Islam is thought to enter the fetus after four months; therefore, abortion after that time is considered murder and is usually condemned. Abortion before that time, al-Kawthari contends, may be acceptable in some cases such as those involving the mental or physical health of the mother or the child.

As you read, consider the following questions:

1. According to al-Kawthari, what do some scholars say is required in a "genuine" situation of need that makes it impossible to terminate a pregnancy to protect the mother's life?
2. How does the author explain why aborting a fetus before one hundred and twenty days, while not considered murder, is still considered unlawful?
3. According to al-Kawthari, is it lawful to abort a fetus conceived in a rape after one hundred and twenty days have passed?

Muhammad ibn Adam al-Kawthari, *Birth Control & Abortion in Islam*, Santa Barbara, CA: White Thread Press, 2006, pp. 50–57, 60–63, 65–67. Copyright © Muhammad Ibn Adam Al-Kawthari 2006. All rights reserved. Reproduced by permission.

It is a well-established principle of Islam that Allāh Almighty has honored human beings. . . .

Thus, it is unlawful (*harām*) to transgress in any way against human life, for it is sacred. Killing a human is considered one of the greatest of sins in the sight of Allāh Most High. . . .

The life of a baby within its mother's womb is as sacred as the life of a mother according to the Sharīʿa.

Human Life Is Sacred

The jurists (*fuqahā*) state that in the case of extreme hunger, when there is no alternative available, unlawful things such as pork and alcohol become permissible to consume. However, even in such a situation, consuming or deriving benefit from a human body (cannibalism) remains unlawful. Human beings have been given the highest status of being the noblest of all creatures; hence, the sanctity of human life is beyond that of any other created thing. . . .

The jurists have also stated that if one is forced into killing another human being, it is still impermissible to do so, even if one's own life was in danger. . . .

Human life is sacred, whether that life is extra- or intrauterine, as both are equal and sanctified according to the Sharīʿa [Islamic law]. It does not matter where that life exists, for its location neither adds to nor detracts from its sanctity. The life of a baby within its mother's womb is as sacred as the life of a mother according to the Sharīʿa. Thus, it will be necessary to retain its sanctity. . . .

In conclusion, the human body, unborn, alive, or dead, has great significance. It is honored and sacred, and because of the sanctity attached to it, it is unlawful to terminate it, tamper with it, cut parts of it off, or dishonor it in any way.

The Soul Enters the Fetus

According to the Sharī'a, abortion can be divided into two types: (1) abortion after the soul (rūh) has entered the fetus; and (2) abortion prior to the entry of the soul into the fetus.

It is imperative to know that according to the Sharī'a, the soul enters the fetus at 120 days (four months) from the date of conception. . . .

Thus, when the age of the unborn child reaches 120 days (four months), it no longer remains a lifeless object; rather, it is a living human being. At this point, all organ differentiation is almost completed and the child acquires the shape of a human body.

When the pregnancy reaches 120 days, an abortion becomes totally forbidden (harām) and is tantamount to murder, for it is the taking out of an innocent life and killing the baby in the mother's womb. This is the ruling upon which all the Islamic jurists, past and present, have agreed, unanimously condemning such a ghastly act.

It is imperative to know that according to the Sharī'a, the soul enters the fetus at 120 days (four months) from the day of conception.

Imām Ibn Taymiya (may Allāh have mercy on him) states in his Fatāwā [a religious opinion concerning Islamic law], "Aborting a fetus has been declared unlawful (harām) with the consensus of all the Muslim scholars. It is similar to burying an infant alive as referred to by Allāh Most High in the verse of the Qur'ān [Islamic holy book], 'And when the female infant that was buried alive is asked for what crime she was killed.'"

Female infanticide was prevalent during the days of ignorance (jāhiliyya). The Messenger of Allāh [Muhammad, the Prophet of Islam] commanded that this custom be stopped immediately, and Islam regarded this barbaric act not only un-Islamic but against the very nature of humanity. . . .

Muftī Muhammad Shafīʿ ʿUthmānī (may Allāh have mercy on him) comments . . . : "To abort a pregnancy after 120 days will also come under the domain of infanticide, because the soul is entered into the fetus after this period and thereafter it is a living human being."

As stated previously, all the jurists are unanimous on the impermissibility of aborting a pregnancy after 120 days. . . .

Abortion When the Mother's Life Is Endangered

As stated above, abortion after the expiry of four months is totally unlawful (*harām*) and is held as tantamount to murder. However, the question remains as to whether it is permitted to carry out an abortion (after this stage) in the situation where the mother's life is in serious danger.

Contemporary scholars have differed as to the permissibility of an abortion in such a case. Scholars such as Shaykh Muftī Taqi Usmani of Pakistan, Shaykh Saʿīd Ramadān al-Butī of Damascus, Muftī Zafīr al-Dīn of Dār al-ʿUlūm Deoband, India, and others are of the opinion that even in a situation where the mother's life is in danger, an abortion will not be permitted. . . .

They state that the Sharīʿa does not allow the termination of one life in order to save the life of another. This principle is derived from works of classical jurists who consider it forbidden to transgress upon a human life even for the purpose of saving one's own life. . . .

The jurists have also stated that if one is forced into killing another human, it is not permissible, even if one's own life is in danger. . . .

Moreover, one of the necessary requirements for a situation to be considered a "*genuine*" situation of need is that the need be immediate, not something expected to play out in the future. As such, it will not be permitted to terminate the life of the unborn child because of medical examinations showing the mother's life to be at risk in the future. Hence, according to this group of scholars, an abortion will remain unlawful after the expiry of 120 days even if the mother's life is in danger.

However, some other contemporary scholars have given a dispensation in aborting the pregnancy after 120 days only in the situation where the mother's life is in grave danger. Scholars such as Shaykh Mustafā al-Zarqāʾ, Shaykh Khālid Sayfullāh Rahmānī and others are of the view that an abortion for fear of the mother dying, will be permitted even after the entry of the soul into the fetus. They have based this ruling on the famous juristic principle, which states, "If one is confronted by two evils, one should choose the lesser of the two."

They state that the mother's life may be saved and the fetus aborted, for the mother is established in life, with duties and responsibilities, whereas the unborn child is still in the mother's womb.

As for the statements of the classical scholars with regard to the impermissibility of terminating one life to save another, this is when both lives are equal in existence, which is not the case here. A human who has come into this world has many roles and responsibilities; hence, this human's life is considered complete. On the other hand, the unborn child does not enjoy the same role and responsibility in life and its life cannot be characterized as complete. Therefore, there is a logical distinction between the life of the mother and the life of the unborn child.

If a pregnant woman is suddenly faced with extreme illness and pains, and medical experts are of the opinion that if she is treated, her unborn child will die, then in such a case, the pregnant mother will have to be treated even if that leads to the loss of her unborn child. The underlying reason is that the mother is being medically treated for her illness and pain,

Changes in Abortion Law in Muslim Iran

Under the earlier law, abortion before four months was permitted if the mother's life was at risk, but her husband's consent was mandatory. The new law in Iran [passed in 2005] permits termination of pregnancy during the first four months if the foetus [fetus] is mentally or physically handicapped or if the mother's life is in danger. According to the new law, the woman's consent is sufficient to carry out the abortion. However, three specialists must confirm that the foetus is disabled or the mother has a life-threatening condition. A high proportion of the requests for abortion is made in the first trimester and the new law will facilitate the process when there are genetic disorders or serious maternal disease.

B. Larijani and F. Zahedi,
"Changing Parameters for Abortion in Iran,"
Indian Journal of Medical Ethics,
October–December 2006.
www.issuesinmedicalethics.org.

which is the basic right of every human being. The child being lost is merely natural consequence of treating the mother; hence, this action will not be considered a direct killing of the child. . . .

As for when there is a fear of the mother losing her life while giving birth, none of the classical scholars have given explicit permission to terminate the pregnancy; thus, it would not be allowed in general. However, in an extreme case, one may consult a reliable scholar of knowledge and piety and seek his advice.

Abortion Before Four Months

An abortion prior to four months (120 days) is also unlawful (*harām*) in normal situations according to the majority of classical and contemporary scholars, but it will not be classified as murder. . . .

It is worth remembering here that the reason why abortion prior to the soul entering the body is also not permitted is that the fetus is considered to be part of the mother's body. Just as one's very own life and also all the limbs and organs of the human body are a trust given by the Almighty Creator, so too is the fetus a trust given to the mother by Allāh; hence she will not have a right to abort it.

The only difference here is that the sin of aborting the fetus will be of a lesser degree than aborting it after 120 days. It would not be regarded as murder, rather violating the rights of a human organ entrusted to the mother by Allāh Most High.

An abortion prior to four months . . . is also unlawful . . . in normal situations . . . but it will not be classified as murder.

Some contemporary scholars have stated that abortion is permissible as long as it is carried out before the forty days of gestation. But this, however, is incorrect. . . . The permission given by some classical jurists to abort the pregnancy, whether before forty days or 120 days, always pertains to the situation where one has a genuine and valid excuse. Without such an excuse, abortion will remain unlawful at all stages, including before forty days.

The above ruling with regard to abortion before the passing of four months is in ordinary circumstances. However, Islam is a religion of mercy and does not command anything that is beyond the capability of an individual. Allāh Most High says:

Allāh does not burden a soul except that which it can bear.

Based on the above verse of the Qur'ān and other such texts of the Qur'ān and Sunna [the sayings and habits of Muhammad], the jurists have given a dispensation in carrying out an abortion prior to the elapsing of 120 days if there is a genuine and Islamically valid reason.

The famous juristic principle (*qā'ida fiqhiyya*) based on the guidelines of the Qur'ān and Sunna states, "Necessity makes the prohibited lawful." . . .

Imām Haskafī (may Allāh have mercy on him) states, "Aborting the pregnancy is permissible for a valid reason, provided the fetus has not yet been formed." . . .

Imām Ibn 'Ābidīn (may Allāh have mercy on him) gives an example for a valid excuse by stating, "[Haskafī's statement] 'Abortion will be permissible for a valid reason,' such as when the milk of a pregnant woman ceases and the father of the child is not in a position financially to hire a wet nurse, and there is a fear of the child perishing, they [the jurists] state that it will be permissible to terminate the pregnancy . . . provided that the period of 120 days has not elapsed. This is permissible because the fetus has not yet developed into a human, and by aborting it we are saving a human life."

Valid Excuses According to Islam

Therefore, it will be permitted to have an abortion (prior to 120 days) if there is an Islamically valid excuse. These excuses are of two types: (1) those that affect the mother and (2) those that affect the unborn child.

Excuses that affect the mother are (a) the pregnancy constitutes a danger to the mother's physical health; (b) the pregnancy constitutes a danger to the mother's mental health; (c) the pregnancy is caused by rape; and (d) the pregnant woman is severely crippled or suffers from a serious mental illness and is in no position to care for herself, let alone a child, then, if it is possible to place the child for adoption after it is born, an abortion will not be permissible. However, if no such arrangement can be made, it will be permissible to terminate the pregnancy.

Many contemporary scholars have stated that if upon medical examination, it is determined that the child will suffer from severe disabilities or will be inflicted by genetic diseases that will cause the child relentless pains, and that the child will be an undue burden for its parents, then it will be permissible to terminate the pregnancy, but again, provided the four months (120 days) have not passed.

Pregnancy due to illegitimate sexual intercourse cannot be considered a valid excuse for carrying out an abortion.

It should be remembered here though that an abortion would not be justified due to minor reasons and excuses. Thus, there should be a certain danger to the pregnant mother or the unborn baby. Mere doubts will not justify the act of aborting the fetus. Moreover, an honest, reliable, and qualified Muslim doctor must advise this. It would be better if a team of specialists, rather than just one person, decides this. One should consult a reliable scholar to confirm the particulars of one's case, for caution should be exercised in all matters related to the lawful and unlawful.

Pregnancy due to illegitimate sexual intercourse cannot be considered a valid excuse for carrying out an abortion. Islam condemns and rejects illicit sex and everything that may lead to it. . . .

Nevertheless, it would not be permitted to have an abortion due to unlawful sex, regardless of how many days have elapsed in the pregnancy. An abortion is not the appropriate Islamic answer to illegitimate sex that results in pregnancy; rather, the solution is to eradicate the means that lead to fornication. If the door is left open for aborting pregnancies that occur outside of wedlock, the ensuing consequences could be destructive. . . .

The unborn child in the mother's womb is in no way considered a participant in the sin that led to its conception. Hence, it is a severe crime to abort it for the sin of another. It is inhumane and unjust that the unborn child has to pay the price for a sin committed by two people out of wedlock—a sin they desire to conceal from others. One individual cannot bear the burden of another, and every individual must bear his or her own responsibility. . . .

It is clear, then, that an abortion due to illegitimate sexual intercourse cannot be justified. It will remain unlawful after and prior to the soul being entered into the fetus.

Having said that, in some extreme cases an abortion may be permitted. For instance, suppose a young girl below the age of consent is seduced by a mature man and falls pregnant. Would it be permissible in such a case for her to abort the pregnancy and return to her childhood routines or would an abortion still remain unlawful?

Many scholars at the Islamic Fiqh Academy of India are of the view that rape is sufficient grounds to justify abortion because classical jurists have permitted abortion for reasons of lesser significance.

At times, a young girl would prefer suicide rather than give birth to a child conceived out of wedlock. Others may well even leave the religion of Islam altogether if the pregnancy was carried to its full term. All of these are real problems faced by Muslims; hence, a blanket ruling cannot be issued. Each individual case must be taken to a reliable scholar whose knowledge and piety one trusts, and his advice should be sought. . . .

Rape is a sexual crime and is in opposition to adultery and fornication, in the fundamental sense that it is characterized by aggression, force, noncompliance, and violence, whereas unlawful sex is carried out with the consent of both partners. In the unfortunate event of rape, the victim should first resort to immediate medical treatment in order to prevent pregnancy. However, if the pregnancy occurs, then in such a case, many contemporary scholars have permitted terminating the pregnancy provided the stage of the soul being entered into the fetus has not elapsed (120 days).

Many scholars at the Islamic Fiqh Academy of India are of the view that rape is sufficient grounds to justify abortion because classical jurists have permitted abortion for reasons of lesser significance. They state that if a woman is in such a condition of stress and shock that it is impossible for her to face anyone and that she is extremely hurt, it will be permissible for her to abort the pregnancy prior to the passing of 120 days, as this will be considered a genuine and valid reason. In reality, it would be immensely difficult for a woman to be comfortable with a child born out of such a traumatic experience.

Judaism's Approach to Abortion Is neither Pro-Choice nor Pro-Life

Daniel Eisenberg

Daniel Eisenberg is a doctor with the Department of Radiology at Albert Einstein Medical Center in Philadelphia, Pennsylvania. He lectures and teaches on the subject of medical ethics. In the following viewpoint, he argues that Jewish law on abortion does not fit easily into either pro-choice or pro-life philosophies. According to Eisenberg, Jewish law sees the fetus as a potential human being. Therefore, abortion is a very serious matter. It may, however, be permitted in certain situations, such as when the physical or mental well-being of the mother is threatened.

As you read, consider the following questions:

1. What is the punishment in the Torah for causing a woman to miscarry?

2. According to Eisenberg, a fetus that threatens the life of a mother is considered tantamount to what in Jewish law?

3. Why do most rabbis forbid abortions in cases of abnormalities or deformities in the fetus?

Ａs abortion resurfaces as a political issue in the upcoming U.S. presidential election [in 2004], it is worthwhile to investigate the Jewish approach to the issue. The traditional Jewish view of abortion does not fit conveniently into any of the major "camps" in the current American abortion debate. We neither ban abortion completely nor do we allow indiscriminate abortion "on demand."

A woman may feel that until the fetus is born, it is a part of her body, and therefore she retains the right to abort an unwanted pregnancy. Does Judaism recognize a right to "choose" abortion? In what situations does Jewish law sanction abortion?

Almost Human

To gain a clear understanding of when abortion is permitted (or even required) and when it is forbidden requires an appreciation of certain nuances of *halacha* (Jewish law) that govern the status of the fetus.

The easiest way to conceptualize a fetus in *halacha* is to imagine it as a full-fledged human being—but not quite. In most circumstances, the fetus is treated like any other "person." Generally, one may not deliberately harm a fetus. But while it would seem obvious that Judaism holds accountable one who purposefully causes a woman to miscarry, sanctions are even placed upon one who strikes a pregnant woman causing an unintentional miscarriage. That is not to say that all rabbinical authorities consider abortion to be murder. The fact that the Torah [the body of wisdom and law contained in Jewish scripture] requires a monetary payment for causing a miscarriage is interpreted by some rabbis to indicate that abortion is not a capital crime and by others as merely indicating that one is not executed for performing an abortion, even though it is a type of murder. . . . Nevertheless, it is universally agreed that the fetus will become a full-fledged human being and there must be a very compelling reason to allow for abortion.

As a general rule, abortion in Judaism is permitted only if there is a direct threat to the life of the mother by carrying the fetus to term or through the act of childbirth. In such a circumstance, the baby is considered tantamount to a *rodef*, a pursuer after the mother with the intent to kill her. Nevertheless, as explained in the Mishna, [the first major written collection of the oral traditions of Judaism] if it would be possible to save the mother by maiming the fetus, such as by amputating a limb, abortion would be forbidden. Despite the classification of the fetus as a pursuer, once the baby's head or most of its body has been delivered, the baby's life is considered equal to the mother's, and we may not choose one life over another, because it is considered as though they are both pursuing each other.

It is universally agreed that the fetus will become a full-fledged human being and there must be a very compelling reason to allow for abortion.

It is important to point out that the reason that the life of the fetus is subordinate to the mother is because the fetus is the *cause* of the mother's life-threatening condition, whether directly (e.g., due to toxemia, placenta previa, or breach position) or indirectly (e.g., exacerbation of underlying diabetes, kidney disease, or hypertension). A fetus may not be aborted to save the life of any other person whose life is not directly threatened by the fetus, such as use of fetal organs for transplant.

Psychiatric Threats

Judaism recognizes psychiatric as well as physical factors in evaluating the potential threat that the fetus poses to the

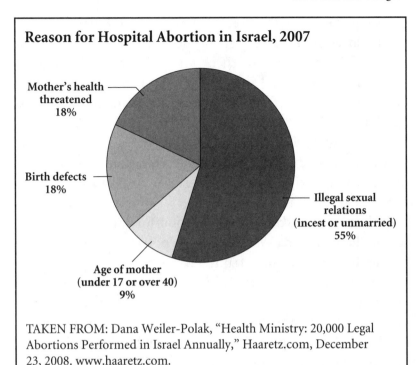

Reason for Hospital Abortion in Israel, 2007

Mother's health threatened 18%

Birth defects 18%

Illegal sexual relations (incest or unmarried) 55%

Age of mother (under 17 or over 40) 9%

TAKEN FROM: Dana Weiler-Polak, "Health Ministry: 20,000 Legal Abortions Performed in Israel Annually," Haaretz.com, December 23, 2008. www.haaretz.com.

mother. However, the danger posed by the fetus (whether physical or emotional) must be both probable and substantial to justify abortion. The degree of mental illness that must be present to justify termination of a pregnancy has been widely debated by rabbinic [that is by Jewish religious] scholars, without a clear consensus of opinions regarding the exact criteria for permitting abortion in such instances. Nevertheless, all agree that were a pregnancy to cause a woman to become truly suicidal, there would be grounds for abortion. However, several modern rabbinical experts ruled that since pregnancy-induced and postpartum depressions are treatable, abortion is not warranted.

As a rule, Jewish law does not assign relative values to different lives. Therefore, . . . most major *poskim* (rabbis qualified to decide matters of Jewish law) forbid abortion in cases of abnormalities or deformities found in a fetus. Rabbi Moshe

Feinstein, one [of] the greatest poskim of the past century, rules that even amniocentesis [a medical test in which amniotic fluid is withdrawn to check for fetal abnormalities, especially Down syndrome] is forbidden if it is performed only to evaluate for birth defects for which the parents might request an abortion. Nevertheless, a test may be performed if a permitted action may result, such as performance of amniocentesis or drawing alpha-fetoprotein [a protein in fetuses] levels for improved peripartum [during labor] or postpartum [after pregnancy] medical management.

While most *poskim* forbid abortion for "defective" fetuses, Rabbi Eliezer Yehuda Waldenberg is a notable exception. Rabbi Waldenberg allows first trimester abortion of a fetus that would be born with a deformity that would cause it to suffer, and termination of a fetus with a lethal fetal defect such as Tay-Sachs [a disease that usually results in the death of the child by age six] up to the seventh month of gestation. The rabbinic experts also discuss the permissibility of abortion for mothers with German measles and babies with prenatal confirmed Down syndrome.

As a rule, Jewish law does not assign relative values to different lives. Therefore . . . most major poskim *(rabbis qualified to decide matters of Jewish law) forbid abortion in cases of abnormalities or deformities found in a fetus.*

Adultery, Rape, and Incest

There is a difference of opinion regarding abortion for adultery or in other cases of impregnation from a relationship with someone biblically forbidden. In cases of rape and incest, a key issue would be the emotional toll exacted from the mother in carrying the fetus to term. In cases of rape, Rabbi Shlomo Zalman Auerbach allows the woman to use methods that prevent pregnancy after intercourse. The same analysis used in other cases of emotional harm might be applied here.

Cases of adultery interject additional considerations into the debate, with rulings ranging from prohibition to it being a mitzvah [good deed] to abort.

I have attempted to distill the essence of the traditional Jewish approach to abortion. Nevertheless, every woman's case is unique and special, and the parameters determining the permissibility of abortion within *halacha* are subtle and complex. It is crucial to remember that when faced with an actual patient, a competent halachic authority must be consulted in every case.

Catholics Can Support a Pro-Choice Stand on Abortion

Jon O'Brien and Sara Morello

Jon O'Brien is the president and Sara Morello is the vice president of Catholics for Choice (formerly known as Catholics for a Free Choice), an organization for pro-choice Catholics, based in Washington, D.C. In the following viewpoint, the authors argue that Catholics may support the choice to have an abortion. As evidence, they note that Catholic teaching on abortion has been inconsistent, and that freedom of individual conscience is a central Catholic value. They also note that part of what makes a teaching valid in the church community is its reception by the members and a large percentage of Catholics have rejected the teaching of the church hierarchy on contraception and abortion.

As you read, consider the following questions:

1. Who is cited by O'Brien and Morello as an authority for obeying conscience over church teaching?

2. What are the ontological and perversity views on abortion, according to the authors?

3. What three teachings have been declared infallible by the Catholic hierarchy, according to O'Brien and Morello?

We strive to be an expression of Catholicism as it is lived by ordinary people. We are part of the great majority of the faithful in the Catholic Church who disagree with the dictates of the Vatican on matters related to sexuality, contraception and abortion.

In all parts of the world, women, men and their families suffer and some die because they lack the resources to plan their families and the comprehensive information and education to keep themselves safe and healthy. The Catholic hierarchy's role in influencing public policy affects everyone—Catholic and non-Catholic—by limiting the availability of reproductive health services worldwide. The Catholic hierarchy's lobbying against contraception and abortion has disastrous effects on women's lives both in the US [United States] and abroad and especially on the lives of poor women.

We believe in a world where every woman and man has access to quality and choice in contraception. Wherever possible, we believe in working to reduce the incidence of unplanned and unwanted pregnancy and that society and individuals should strive to give women and men real choices.

We believe that social services should exist in our communities . . . where no one is ever forced for any reason to have an abortion or forced to give birth.

We believe that young and old should have access to the best information so we know and understand our bodies and can make the best and most responsible decisions to enjoy and share our sexuality.

We believe that social services should exist in our communities where people can freely access quality health care and child care—where women and men have real choices and where no one is ever forced for any reason to have an abortion or forced to give birth. We believe that women should have access to abortion when they need it, and when, in consultation with their doctors, it can be performed safely.

We work for a world where all women and men are trusted to make responsible decisions about their lives, where skilled and compassionate doctors, nurses and health care providers are allowed and supported in the work they do to enable people to exercise their right to choose.

We are part of the great majority who believe that the teaching on the primacy of conscience means that every individual must follow his or her own conscience—and respect the rights of others to do the same.

We affirm that the moral capacity and the human right to make choices about whether and when to become pregnant or to end a pregnancy are supported by church teachings. We believe that people should be empowered and given support to exercise their rights and responsibilities. We believe that women have a right to choose.

Abortion and Moral Decision-Making

Church teachings on moral decision-making and abortion are complex. In Catholic theology there is room for the acceptance of policies that favor access to the full range of reproductive health options, including contraception and abortion.

At the heart of church teachings on moral matters is a deep regard for an individual's conscience. The *Catechism [of the Catholic Church]* states that "a human being must always obey the certain judgment of his conscience." The church takes conscience so seriously that Richard McBrien, in his essential study *Catholicism*, explained that even in cases of a conflict with the moral teachings of the church, Catholics "not only may but must follow the dictates of conscience rather than the teachings of the Church."

Casual disagreement is not sufficient grounds for ignoring moral teachings. Catholics are obliged to know and consider thoughtfully Catholic teaching. Catholics believe that "the

Church . . . is a major resource of . . . moral direction and leadership. It is the product of centuries of experience, crossing cultural, national, and continental lines" (*Catholicism*, HarperCollins, 1994). But in the end, a well-formed conscience reigns.

Catholic Teachings on Abortion Have Changed over Time

Although the Catholic hierarchy says that the prohibition on abortion is both "unchanged" and "unchangeable," this does not comport with the actual history of abortion teaching, and dissent, within the church.

The *Catechism* contains only six paragraphs on abortion. This brief section starts: "Since the first century the Church has affirmed the moral evil of every procured abortion. This teaching has not changed and remains unchangeable."

While the Catholic Church has long taught that abortion is a sin, the reasons for judging abortion sinful have changed over time. In fact, through most of history the church did not pay much attention to abortion except as a sexual issue. The early prohibition of abortion was not based on concern about the fetus. It was based on a view that only people who engage in forbidden sexual activity would attempt abortion and that abortion is wrong from either an ontological perspective or from a negative judgment about sexuality and sexual behavior, known as the perversity view. "The ontological view is that the human fetus is a person from the earliest moments of conception, hence to abort it is either murder or something closely approximating murder; the perversity view is that sex is only licit within marriage and for the primary purpose of having children, hence abortion perverts sex and is immoral in the same way that contraception is immoral" (*A Brief, Liberal, Catholic Defense of Abortion*, University of Illinois Press, 2000).

The perversity view is no longer much argued explicitly in the Catholic Church, though it underlies many of the hierarchy's arguments. Many church officials and anti-choice Catholics now focus on the ontological view, which argues that the fetus is a person from the moment of conception. This view, however, is based on faulty science, dating from the 17th century, when scientists, looking at fertilized eggs through magnifying glasses and primitive microscopes, imagined that they saw tiny, fully formed animal fetuses.

The church hierarchy has since rejected the notion that a fetus is a fully formed person. In its last statement on abortion, the 1974 *Declaration on Procured Abortion*, the Vatican acknowledged that it does not know when the fetus becomes a person: "There is not a unanimous tradition on this point and authors are as yet in disagreement." This disagreement has a long history as well; neither St. Augustine nor St. Thomas Aquinas, two of the most important theologians in the Catholic tradition, considered the fetus in the early stages of pregnancy to be a person.

The US Supreme Court explored fetal personhood at some length in its *Roe v. Wade* decision and concluded: "When those trained in the respective disciplines of medicine, philosophy and theology are unable to arrive at any consensus, the judiciary, at this point in the development of man's knowledge, is not in a position to speculate as to the answer."

In its last statement on abortion, the 1974 Declaration on Procured Abortion, *the Vatican acknowledged that it does not know when the fetus becomes a person. . . .*

Even in a predominantly Catholic country, laws governing access to abortion need not adhere to the official Catholic position. The Second Vatican Council's *Declaration on Religious Freedom* reinforced the call for Catholics to respect the positions of people of other faiths. This is particularly significant given that the Catholic Church's positions on health policies, including abortion, is more conservative than that of other major faith groups. In addition, as noted, many Catholics do not support the Vatican's position on abortion.

Sound public policy on abortion would affirm respect for developing life without diminishing respect for women's lives. Catholics can and do support public policies that acknowledge the moral agency of women, respect developing life, and appreciate the Catholic tradition while honoring the views of other faith groups.

Church Teachings May Not Be Imposed

Despite what many think, the Vatican may not impose teachings on an unwilling faithful. Through the concept of reception, Catholics have a role to play in the establishment of church law.

The popular notion that whatever the pope says on a serious topic is infallible is an exaggeration of the principle of infallibility. While some ultraconservative groups claim that the teaching on abortion is infallible, it does not in fact meet the definition of an infallible teaching. Since the doctrine of papal infallibility was first declared in 1870, only three teachings have been declared infallible: the Immaculate Conception of Mary; the Assumption of Mary; and the declaration on infallibility itself.

Before the encyclical *Evangelium Vitae* (*The Gospel of Life*) was published in 1995, there was speculation among theologians and others that Pope John Paul II would assert the infallibility of the teaching on abortion. Then cardinal Joseph Ratzinger, the Vatican's chief doctrinal officer, confirmed that the word infallible had been considered in early drafts but was rejected. Ratzinger explained that while the teaching on abortion is authoritative and deserves obedience, the encyclical stopped short of the "formality of dogmatization" (*National Catholic Reporter*, April 7, 1995).

Moral Acceptability of Issues, Among Catholics and Non-Catholics, 2006–2008

	% morally acceptable Catholics	Non-Catholics
	%	%
Abortion	40	41
Death penalty	61	68
Sex between an unmarried man and woman	67	57
Divorce	71	66
Medical research using stem cells obtained from human embryos	63	62
Having a baby outside of marriage	61	52
Gambling	72	59
Homosexual relations	54	45

Frank Newport,
"Catholics Similar to Mainstream on Abortion, Stem Cells,"
Gallup.com, March 30, 2009. www.gallup.com.

The teaching authority of the church is not based solely on statements of the hierarchy; it also includes the scholarly efforts of theologians and the lived experience of Catholic people. "Since the Church is a living body," the Vatican declared in the 1971 *Communio et Progressio*, "she needs public opinion in order to sustain a giving and taking between her members. Without this, she cannot advance in thought and action."

There is a diversity of opinion among leading theologians on the Vatican's teaching on abortion. As long ago as 1973, noted Catholic theologian Charles Curran wrote in the *Jurist* that "there is a sizable and growing number of Catholic theologians who do disagree with some aspects of the officially proposed Catholic teaching that direct abortion from the time of conception is always wrong."

The importance of lay Catholics' experience in the establishment of church law is recognized through the concept of reception. Leading canon lawyer James Coriden shows how the principle of reception, "asserts that for a [church] law or rule to be an effective guide for the believing community it must be accepted by that community." Through the centuries, church law experts have reaffirmed an understanding that "the obligatory force of church law is affected by its reception by the community."

The teaching authority of the church is not based solely on statements of the hierarchy; it also includes the scholarly efforts of theologians and the lived experience of Catholic people.

Like the concept of the primacy of conscience, the principle of reception does not mean that Catholic law is to be taken lightly or rejected without thoughtful and prudent consideration. Coriden writes, "reception is not a demonstration of popular sovereignty or an outcropping of populist democracy. It is a legitimate participation by the people in their own governance."

Many of the hierarchy's teachings on reproductive health and rights have not been received by the faithful. Rather, Catholics all over the world have soundly rejected the church's ban on contraception and in many countries only a minority of Catholics agree with church leaders on abortion.

Barely a fifth (22%) of Catholics in the US agree with the bishops that abortion should be completely illegal, and Catholic women in the US have abortions at the same rate as women in the population as a whole. Majorities of Catholics in Bolivia (66%), Colombia (54%) and Mexico (69%) feel abortion should be permitted under some or all circumstances. In Italy, which is 97 percent Catholic, 74 percent favor the use of RU-486 (a drug used instead of surgical methods in some early abortions).

When it comes to the Vatican's teachings on abortion, Catholics the world over stand well apart from the hierarchy.

Conclusion

Church teachings, tradition and core Catholic tenets—including the primacy of conscience, the role of the faithful in defining legitimate laws and norms, and support for the separation of church and state—leave room for supporting a more liberal position on abortion. The church has acknowledged that it does not know when the fetus becomes a person and has never declared its position on abortion to be infallible. Catholics can, in good conscience, support access to abortion and affirm that abortion can be a moral choice. Indeed, many of us do.

Catholic Legislators Who Support Abortion Should Be Denied Communion

Pete Vere

Pete Vere is a Canadian Catholic writer and canon lawyer. In the following viewpoint, he argues that the Roman Catholic Church should deal forcefully with pro-choice legislators. Automatic excommunication is not supported by Catholic law; instead, excommunication would require a lengthy and difficult judicial process. Canon law, however, does allow priests to deny automatically Communion to pro-choice legislators. This denial of Communion is also supported by recent declarations of Pope Benedict XVI.

As you read, consider the following questions:

1. According to Vere, what would a pro-abortion Catholic politician have to have done in order to be automatically excommunicated?
2. What purpose does denying Holy Communion to pro-choice Catholic politicians serve, according to Vere?
3. According to Vere, why does Pope Benedict's mind affect the interpretation of canon law?

Pope Benedict XVI spent part of May [2007] bearing witness to the culture of life. As reported by the CBC [Canadian Broadcasting Corporation]:

> Roman Catholic politicians who support a proposed law allowing women to have abortions in Mexico City should no longer receive Communion, the pope said in a statement clarifying earlier remarks . . .

> "It's nothing new, it's normal, it wasn't arbitrary. It is what is foreseen by the church's doctrine," the pope responded ("No Communion for Pro-Abortion Politicians, Pope Says," CBC News, May 9, 2007).

While the need for strong measures is never a happy moment, the church simply cannot afford inaction when human life lies in the balance. As both a canon lawyer and a political commentator, I am often asked what options are available for dealing with pro-abortion politicians who claim to be Catholic.

Canon 1398 and Canon 915

In the past, I argued for denial of Holy Communion [a Catholic sacrament involving the sharing of a consecrated wafer, called the host]. As much as I felt excommunication was the more appropriate penalty, Canon 1398 [church law number 1398] was clear: "A person who actually procures an abortion incurs a latae sententiae [automatic] excommunication." One of the oldest principles of canon law [church law] is that penalties must be interpreted restrictively. Thus, a pro-abortion Catholic politician was off the excommunication hook unless he or she directly procured an abortion, or acted directly as an accomplice in the procurement of a specific abortion.

Excommunicating pro-abortion Catholic politicians would require a formal judicial process—it could not be carried out automatically. Proving the case would be difficult, and the process would not resolve itself until after election day.

In contrast, invoking Canon 915 is much easier. "Those who obstinately persist in manifest grave sin, are not to be admitted to Holy Communion," the canon states. The *Catechism of the Catholic Church* is also clear: Abortion "is gravely contrary to the moral law" and an "abominable crime." Hence, those who promote and defend abortion, and not merely those who assist in its direct procurement, engage in objectively sinful activity.

No canonical trial is necessary. Any courageous minister of Holy Communion can invoke the canon to deny a pro-abortion Catholic politician Holy Communion, provided his or her diocesan bishop was willing to withstand the accompanying media outrage. It generally accomplishes the same purpose as excommunication—that is, it puts pressure on the offending Catholic to repent, and it sends a clear message to the greater community that certain behaviour will not be tolerated by the Catholic Church.

Those who promote and defend abortion, and not merely those who assist in its direct procurement, engage in objectively sinful activity.

The Pope's Role as Legislator

Let us return to Pope Benedict's May 9 statement. There is some ambiguity in the media reports as to whether His Holiness was speaking of excommunication, or denial of Holy Communion.

Regardless of this, the Holy Father has done more than merely support the Mexican bishops[, who in 2007 threatened pro-choice Catholic legislators with excommunication]. He has revealed his mind as the church's supreme legislator. Granted, his views appear nearly identical to those he expressed while still the prefect for the Congregation for the Doctrine of the Faith [the official office Cardinal Joseph Ratz-

> ## Abortion and Excommunication in Mexico
>
> Pope Benedict XVI began his first trip to Latin America . . . by laying down church law on abortion, suggesting that he agrees with bishops who said Catholic politicians in Mexico had excommunicated themselves by legalizing abortion in that nation's capital.
>
> Benedict . . . also spoke strongly against abortion during his first speech in Brazil. . . . He said he's certain that the bishops will reinforce "the promotion of respect for life from the moment of conception until natural death as an integral requirement of human nature."
>
> *Associated Press,*
> *"Pope Condemns Abortion on Latin America Trip,"*
> *MSNBC Online, May 9, 2007. www.msn.com*

inger held before being elevated to pope in 2005]. Nevertheless, it is one thing to express his opinion as Cardinal Ratzinger, quite another to speak as the successor to St. Peter [that is, as pope].

The response to pro-abortion politicians when they approach the altar is to deny them Holy Communion.

As the church's supreme legislator, Pope Benedict's mind affects how the laws are to be interpreted. Canon 16 [section] 1 is clear: "Laws are authentically interpreted by the legislator. . . . If the meaning [of a law] remains doubtful or obscure." Canon 17 adds, "there must be recourse to . . . the mind of the legislator." With the passing of Pope John Paul II, who promulgated the Code of Canon Law, the burden now falls upon his successor, Pope Benedict, to provide us with the mind of the legislator.

Pope Benedict states that denying Holy Communion to pro-abortion Catholic politicians is nothing new. He is saying this is the normal response of the Catholic Church, in keeping with her doctrine and the natural law. Thus, a question is answered. In keeping with the mind of Pope Benedict XVI, the church's Supreme Legislator, the response to pro-abortion politicians when they approach the altar is to deny them Holy Communion.

Periodical Bibliography

The following articles have been selected to supplement the diverse views presented in this chapter.

BBC	"Buddhism and Abortion," November 23, 2009. www.bbc.co.uk.
BBC	"Hinduism and Abortion," August 25, 2009. www.bbc.co.uk.
Maya Berezovsky	"Controversy 101: Abortion and Judaism," *KOACH-on-Campus*, March 9, 2005. www.koach.org.
Tom Ehrich	"Where Does God Stand on Abortion?" *USA Today*, August 13, 2006. www.usatoday.com.
M. Junaid Levesque-Alam	"Islam, Abortion, and the Stupak Amendment," NAM Ethnoblog, November 25, 2009. http://ethnoblog.newamericamedia.org.
Vasu Murti and Mary Krane Derr	"Abortion Is Bad Karma: Hindu Perspectives," *Feminism and Nonviolence Studies*, Fall 1998. www.fnsa.org.
National Public Radio	"Catholic Church Stokes Political Debate on Abortion, Gay Marriage," November 25, 2009. www.npr.org.
Rob Phillips	"Survey Examines Protestant Preaching on Marriage, Abortion," *Christian Post*, November 24, 2009. www.christianpost.com.
Alissa J. Rubin	"The Catholic Abortion Paradox," Beliefnet, January 2001. www.beliefnet.com.
Alan Yuter	"The Abortion Rhetoric Within Orthodox Judaism: Consensus, Conviction, Covenant," Institute for Jewish Ideas and Ideals, March 11, 2009. www.jewishideas.org.

GLOBALVIEWPOINTS

CHAPTER 2

Abortion and the Law

In Ireland, Abortion Should Remain Illegal

William Binchy

William Binchy is Regius Professor of Laws at Trinity College Dublin, and is legal adviser to the Pro Life Campaign, an Irish pro-life organization. In the following viewpoint, Binchy addresses the case of Tysiac v. Poland, *in which the European Court of Human Rights ruled that Poland's efforts to restrict abortion violated the individual rights of women. Binchy argues that in making this ruling, the court considered only the rights of mothers and not the rights of unborn children to protection. Irish values, Binchy says, require consideration of the lives of unborn children. The court, he concludes, is trying to impose laws that contradict Irish values.*

As you read, consider the following questions:

1. According to Binchy, on what grounds, and through what legal procedures, has abortion been available under Polish law?
2. Did the court in this case guarantee all Europeans a right to abortion?
3. According to Binchy, what standard of care is provided by Irish maternity hospitals?

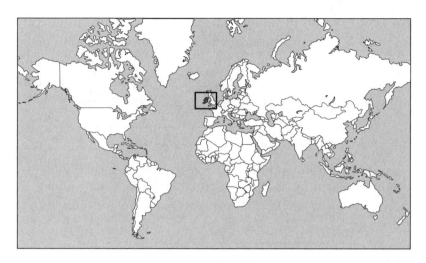

The recent decision of the Chamber Court of the European Court of Human Rights in *Tysiac v. Poland* [2007] is a source of concern to those who would wish the court to give full protection to the human rights of human beings at all stages in their lives. A different, but important, concern that it raises is its failure to respect the diversity of values throughout Europe on this question.

A Clash of Values

The court is not in an easy political situation. If it holds that every human life is worthy of equal protection, regardless of the age or strength or physical or mental capacity of the human being involved, it will run into political conflict with very many European countries whose culture is at variance with this value.

If, on the other hand, it treats some lives as less worthy of protection than others and their right to life as being subject to the right to choose of others, it will force countries who regard all human lives as being of equal worth and dignity to contradict that value in their legal system under pain of being found in violation of the European Convention [on Human Rights].

In the face of this dilemma, the court until now has largely adopted a neutral stance, taking no definitive position on the right to life of unborn children under the convention and leaving it to the states to fashion their legal policy in accordance with their values rather than those of the court.

[The court] will force countries who regard all human lives as being of equal worth and dignity to contradict that value in their legal system under pain of being found in violation of the European Convention [on Human Rights].

Siding Against Pro-Life

The *Tysiac* decision represents a radical shift in the court's approach. The court has entered the debate, in substance though not formally, in a way that reduces protection for unborn children.

Under Polish law, abortion is an offence unless carried out in accordance with legislation of 1993, which authorises abortions carried out for a number of specified grounds, including endangerment of the mother's life or health. A certificate of a physician other than the one carrying out the abortion is required, save in cases involving a direct threat to the mother's life.

The pregnant woman does not herself incur criminal liability for an abortion carried out in contravention of the 1993 act.

Ms [Alicja] Tysiac's complaint, to which the court adhered, was that the failure by Polish law to provide a procedural framework to cover a situation where a woman disagreed with the views of medical experts that a condition warranting an abortion did not exist constituted a violation of her right to private life under Article 8 of the convention.

The court (by a six to one majority) stated that it noted that "the legal prohibition on abortion, taken together with the risk of their incurring criminal responsibility under . . . the Criminal Code, can well have a chilling effect on doctors when deciding whether the requirements of legal abortion are met in an individual case.

"The provisions regulating the availability of lawful abortion should be formulated in such a way as to alleviate this effect. Once the legislature decides to allow abortion, it must not structure its legal framework in a way which would limit real possibilities to obtain it."

The court preserved a strand of its formerly neutral approach when, having noted that abortion was lawful on grounds of endangerment of life or health in Poland, it commented: "Hence, it is not the court's task in the present case to examine whether the convention guarantees a right to have an abortion." This leaves to another day the task for the court in confronting whether unborn children have any right to life under Article 2 of the convention [which states that everyone's right to life is protected by law] and, if they do, why it may be less valuable than the right to life of other human beings.

Neutrality has thus given way to a calibration process in which only the rights of the mother are to be taken into account.

No Rights for the Unborn

Yet the tenor of the decision in *Tysiac v. Poland* is to maximise whatever right to abortion may exist in a state's law. In essence, the majority judgment appears to favour the view that, once abortion is part of the law of a state, the court should not engage in any process in which the rights of the unborn are taken into account, but rather that they should be completely discounted because of the court's failure to have clarified the entitlements of unborn children under the conven-

Irish Women Who Travelled to Britain for Abortions, 2000–2008

Abortion is restricted in Ireland. As a result, women who desire abortions often go to neighboring Britain, where abortions are more easily obtained.

Year	Number of Women
2000	6,391
2001	6,673
2002	6,522
2003	6,320
2004	6,217
2005	5,585
2006	5,042
2007	4,686
2008	4,600

Irish Family Planning Association,
"Irish Abortion Statistics," www.ifpa.ie.

tion. Neutrality has thus given way to a calibration process in which only the rights of the mother are to be taken into account.

Let us test this interpretation by examining the implications of the decision on laws, such as in Britain, where there is a ground for abortion based on endangerment of the mother's health, backed by the certificates of two doctors. The reality is that these signatures are very easy to obtain.

If a true concern for the protection of the rights of unborn children were the basis of the court's decision, then there would have to be procedural rules which made it possible for unborn children to be protected from certificates provided by doctors which authorised abortion where in truth the mother's health was not endangered.

Yet we know that this is not what the court intended. What emerges is thus a one-sided concern for protection of rights which will surely have a chilling effect on doctors who might be disposed to decline to authorise an abortion.

Consequences for Ireland

What are the implications for Ireland? At present, the position is that the Supreme Court interpreted the law in such a way as to present no procedural barriers to abortion, up to birth, on a substantive basis that extended to a threat of suicide. This leaves the unborn child inadequately protected under law, though thankfully not under medical ethics.

Irish people should not be obliged to have forced on them a law that contradicts their values regarding human dignity and equal worth.

Our maternity hospitals deliver the highest international standards of care for mother and child, far better than a range of countries with more resources and a liberal abortion regime. Our doctors, in protecting the lives of both patients, demonstrate in the most important practical way that it is better not to ignore the unborn child.

The decision in *Tysiac v. Poland* has made that mistake. Irish people should not be obliged to have forced on them a law that contradicts their values regarding human dignity and equal worth by a court which operates politically on a Pan-European stage. We should be entitled to insist that our legal culture respect the unique value of every human life, with the practical implications that this involves for our social and economic policies, so that a genuinely caring society of solidarity and support is achieved.

In Europe, Abortion Should Be Legalized

Gisela Wurm

Gisela Wurm is an Austrian appointee to the Parliamentary Assembly of the Council of Europe (PACE), an international body that advises European member states. In the following viewpoint, she acts as investigator and reporter for the Committee on Equal Opportunities for Women and Men, which formulates policy recommendations for the European Commission. In this capacity, Wurm argues that banning abortion does not reduce the number of abortions, but instead leads to unsafe, illegal procedures. Therefore, she concludes, bans and restrictions on abortions should be eliminated throughout Europe.

As you read, consider the following questions:

1. What are the only countries in Europe where abortion is not permitted, even to save the life of the mother?

2. According to Wurm, what negative effects of abortion are emphasized by the pro-life camp?

3. According to Wurm, which nation has the highest contraception rate in the world?

Gisela Wurm, "Access to Safe and Legal Abortion in Europe," *PACE News*, Doc. 11537, March 17, 2008.

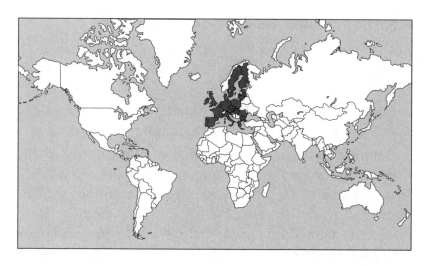

Abortion is legal in the vast majority of the Council of Europe member states. The Committee on Equal Opportunities for Women and Men considers that a ban on abortions does not result in fewer abortions, but mainly leads to clandestine abortions, which are more traumatic and more dangerous. By the same token, the committee notes that in many of the states where abortion is legal, numerous conditions are imposed which restrict the effective access to safe abortion.

The Parliamentary Assembly [the legislative body of the Council of Europe] should therefore invite the member states of the Council of Europe to:

- decriminalise abortion, if they have not already done so;

- guarantee women's effective exercise of their right to abortion and lift restrictions which hinder, de jure [by right] or de facto [in reality], access to safe abortion;

- adopt appropriate sexual and reproductive health strategies, including access of women and men to contraception at a reasonable cost and of a suitable nature for them as well as compulsory relationships and sex education for young people.

Abortion Should Be Rare but Accessible

The Parliamentary Assembly reaffirms that abortion can in no circumstances be regarded as a family planning method. Abortion must, as far as possible, be avoided. All possible means compatible with women's rights must be used to reduce the number of both unwanted pregnancies and abortions.

Although abortion is legal in the vast majority of the Council of Europe member states, the Assembly is concerned that, in many of these states, numerous conditions are imposed and restrict the effective access to safe abortion. These restrictions have discriminatory effects, since women who are well informed and possess adequate financial means can often obtain legal and safe abortions more easily.

The Assembly also notes that, in member states where abortion is legal, conditions are not always such as to guarantee women effective access to this right: The lack of local health care facilities, the lack of doctors willing to carry out abortions, the repeated medical consultations required, the time allowed for changing one's mind and the waiting time for the abortion all have the potential to make access to abortion more difficult, or even impossible in practice.

The Parliamentary Assembly reaffirms that abortion can in no circumstances be regarded as a family planning method. Abortion must, as far as possible, be avoided.

The Assembly takes the view that abortion should not be banned. A ban on abortions does not result in fewer abortions, but mainly leads to clandestine abortions, which are more traumatic and more dangerous. The lawfulness of abortion does not have an effect on a woman's need for an abortion, but only on her access to a safe abortion.

At the same time, the Assembly is convinced that appropriate sexual and reproductive health strategies, including compulsory relationships and sex education for young people, contribute to less recourse to abortion.

The Assembly affirms the right of all human beings, women included, to respect for their physical integrity and to freedom to control their own bodies. In this context, the ultimate decision on whether or not to have an abortion should be a matter for the woman concerned, and she should have the means of exercising this right in an effective way.

The Parliamentary Assembly invites the member states of the Council of Europe to:

• decriminalise abortion, if they have not already done so;

• guarantee women's effective exercise of their right to abortion;

• allow women freedom of choice and offer the conditions of a free and enlightened choice;

• lift restrictions which hinder, de jure or de facto, access to safe abortion, and in particular take the necessary steps to create the appropriate conditions for health, medical and psychological care and offer suitable financial cover;

• adopt appropriate sexual and reproductive health strategies based on sound and reliable data, ensuring continued improvements and expansion of contraceptive service provision by increased investments from the national budgets into improving health systems, reproductive health supplies and information provision;

• ensure that women and men have access to contraception at a reasonable cost, of a suitable nature for them, and chosen by them;

- introduce compulsory relationships and sex education for young people (inter alia [among other outlets], in schools), so as to avoid as many unwanted pregnancies (and therefore abortions) as possible.

- promote a more pro-family attitude in public information campaigns. . . .

The Situation in Europe

The situation in Europe regarding abortion is very diverse. Abortion is legal in the vast majority of the Council of Europe member states. In all of the Council of Europe member states, except Andorra and Malta, the law permits abortion in order to save women's lives. Abortion on request is—in theory—available in all Council of Europe member states, except Andorra, Malta, Ireland, and Poland. Some Council of Europe member states enjoy high levels of sexual and reproductive health while some others have some of the highest abortion rates in the world. In some member states, abortion is legal, safe, free and accessible, while in others, women are obliged to resort to illegal and unsafe abortions if they want to terminate a pregnancy. In some countries where abortion is legal (in certain circumstances), abortion is de facto, not accessible, due to reasons such as high prices of abortion, women unfriendly providers, crowded facilities, poor hygienic conditions, poor access to information, lack of proper abortion training and inadequate standards of care.

According to information provided by the International Planned Parenthood Federation (IPPF), abortion rates are generally on the decline in Europe, particularly in the countries of central and eastern Europe. In the European Union, the figures remain stable. However, there is an increase in the abortion rate among younger women. It should be borne in mind though that data collection systems in Europe differ considerably, and not all statistics are reliable, which makes it difficult to be certain of developments.

The legislation varies considerably from country to country in Europe, however: In most cases, an abortion can be requested up to the 12th week; up to 18 weeks in Sweden; up to 22 weeks in most of the Caucasian countries for social or medical reasons; up to 24 weeks in the Netherlands and the United Kingdom in the event of social, medical or economic constraints; only under certain conditions in Cyprus, Luxembourg, Poland, Portugal (the situation is, however, changing in Portugal, where a referendum was held recently) and Spain; only if the mother's life is in danger (Ireland and Northern Ireland); and not at all in Malta.

Access to abortion differs considerably depending on whether women live in urban or rural areas.

A period of reflection is required only in western Europe, not in the former Soviet countries. Counselling in one form or another is mandatory in most west European countries, but not in eastern Europe. When the abortion concerns a minor, parental consent is required in most countries, but not in Belgium. In France, it is recommended that the minor be accompanied by an adult. The cost of an abortion varies from one country to another and depends on the woman's age and social situation. Abortion is often free in eastern Europe. Bulgaria and Kazakhstan offer state financial assistance to poor women and to girls. In Austria, Spain and Portugal, the cost is around 300 to 800 € [about 450 to 1,100 dollars]. In Armenia and Georgia, it is between 15 and 85 € [about 22 to 125 dollars].

Access to abortion differs considerably depending on whether women live in urban or rural areas. In most countries, access to abortion is limited to hospitals: Some have set up specialised departments, but not all hospitals have obstetricians (or qualified doctors) who perform abortions. According to several studies carried out in the Russian Federation, the number of unreported abortions is much higher than that officially registered and adolescents, young, unmarried women and women in rural areas are those who seek unsafe abortion. In some countries, such as Poland, doctors refuse to perform abortions on personal moral grounds. In many countries, the quality of the care given to a woman seeking an abortion leaves much to be desired.

The Pro-Life Argument

We are all very well aware of the moral argument, which has split whole societies (most obviously the United States of America since the famous US Supreme Court decision *Roe v. Wade*) into two camps, which call themselves "pro-life" and "pro-choice". At the risk of restating the obvious, allow me nevertheless briefly to summarise the arguments of both camps:

The "pro-life" camp holds that life begins at conception, not birth, and that the embryo—as a human being—should benefit from human rights, including, of course, the right to life itself. Abortion is thus classified as "murder" or "suppression of human life". Most religions place themselves in the "pro-life" camp according to Mrs [Rosemarie] Zapfl-Helbling's report on "women and religion in Europe" (from which I have taken the following information). The Roman Catholic Church considers abortion a "moral evil", and a breach of the fifth commandment ("You shall not kill."), as human life is to be respected and protected absolutely from the moment of conception. The Orthodox Church condemns abortion as an act of murder in every case. In Islam, abortion is outlawed unless the mother's health or well-being is at risk (and then, it is only permitted during the first 120 days). In Judaism, abortion—in restricted circumstances—is allowed until the 40th day, as the foetus [fetus] is not regarded as an autonomous person. The mainstream Lutheran and Protestant churches are usually more tolerant on abortion, although the more charismatic and fundamentalist churches take a stricter stance.

The "pro-life" camp sees the mother's body as "just the place where the unborn child grows and feeds", and this is why the woman is not seen as having the right to decide on the life of the unborn child. The father's role is also highlighted by "pro-life" activists: Since the child has two parents, not one, why should only one of them be allowed to decide its fate?

The "pro-life" camp emphasises the possible negative effects an abortion can have on a woman: both physically and psychologically ("symptoms comparable with post-traumatic stress disorder, involving nightmares, a feeling of guilt, a need to 'make amends'").

The "pro-life" camp sees the mother's body as "just the place where the unborn child grows and feeds", and this is why the woman is not seen as having the right to decide on the life of the unborn child.

Abortion is not seen as a private matter, in particular in view of current demographic trends. The existence of alternatives to abortion (adoption, foster homes) is stressed.

The Pro-Choice Argument

The "pro-choice" camp holds that "the right to safe abortion should be considered as a fundamental human right". The argument builds on women's right to life and to health, since in countries where abortion is restricted by law women, tend to resort to illegal abortions in conditions which are medically unsafe and put their lives and health at risk. The lawfulness of abortion does not have an effect on a woman's need for an abortion, but only on her access to a safe abortion.

Laws banning abortion are considered by "pro-choice" activists to expose women—not men—to increased health risks

Estimated Abortions per 1,000 Women Aged 15–44 by Region

Region	Abortion Rate 1995	2003
Africa	33	29
Asia	33	29
Europe	48	28
Latin America	37	31
United States and Canada	22	21
Oceania	21	17

Guttmacher Institute,
"Facts on Induced Abortion Worldwide,"
October 2009. www.guttmacher.org

and therefore to have a discriminatory effect. The laws are also seen as discriminatory in that they "both denigrate and undermine women's capacity to make responsible decisions about their lives and their bodies".

Furthermore, women are seen as having a right to reproductive self-determination: According to Ms [Anne] Quesney (director of Abortion Rights, United Kingdom), "going through with an unwanted pregnancy can take a heavy toll on women's physical and emotional well-being and that of their families". Ms Quesney thus considered that it was not the government's role to make decisions in their stead. For women living in settings where family planning and education are unavailable, access to safe abortion services could be the only means of controlling the size of their families. Furthermore, "pro-choice" activists emphasise that no method of contraception is 100% reliable.

The "pro-choice" camp further points out that banning abortion only forces it underground—"making it one of the greatest dangers to women's rights, health, equality and independence", in the words of Ms Quesney. Evidence of the abortion restrictions under [former Communist leader Nicolae] Ceauşescu's Romania proves this link.

Laws banning abortion are considered by "pro-choice" activists to expose women—not men—to increased health risks and therefore to have a discriminatory effect.

Finally, reference should be made to the position adopted by [human rights organization] Amnesty International, which, at its 28th International Council Meeting, in Mexico City on 17 August 2007, turned its attention for the first time to certain aspects of abortion, following wide-ranging consultation of its members, in the context of its "Stop Violence Against Women" campaign:

Amnesty International's policy on sexual and reproductive rights does not promote abortion as a universal right and the organisation remains silent on the rights or wrongs of abortion. The policy recognizes women's human rights to be free of fear, threat and coercion as they manage all consequences of rape and other grave human rights violations. Amnesty International stands by its policy, adopted in April this year, that aims to support the decriminalisation of abortion, to ensure women have access to health care when complications arise from abortion and to defend women's access to abortion—within reasonable gestational limits—when their health or lives are in danger.

In this context, Amnesty International underlined that, "unlike in any other situation, medical service providers will often refuse to treat women suffering from complications related to abortion. There is no analogous treatment, i.e., the denial of medical services because the person in need of medical treatment is perceived or alleged to have committed a crime. People who overdose on drugs that are deemed illegal receive treatment (. . .), but women are denied this treatment, reflecting the exceptionalism around the issue of abortion". This position seems a particularly interesting one, placing the debate in the sphere of the protection of women against all forms of violence, and not in the moral sphere.

Avoiding Abortions

Whatever view we hold on abortion, we can all agree that, in an ideal world, abortions would not exist—not because they were banned, but because they were unnecessary in that, in most cases, they are avoidable. Our aim should thus be to avoid as many abortions as possible.

The best way to avoid abortions is to avoid unwanted pregnancies by offering accessible and affordable contraception, and sex education for young adults (including in schools). As Ms [Katarina] Lindahl from the Swedish Association for Sexuality Education explained at the hearing, WHO [World Health Organization] studies have revealed that sex education has the effect of postponing young people's first sexual relations, increasing the use of contraceptives and making sexual relations safer. A WHO report, *Preventing HIV/ AIDS in Young People*, revealed that education about HIV tended to delay sexual activity, and that sex education did not increase sexual activity. These results can be transposed to unwanted pregnancies.

Whatever view we hold on abortion, we can all agree that, in an ideal world, abortions would not exist . . . in that, in most cases, they are avoidable.

Similarly, the availability of affordable contraception has done much to lower abortion rates over the years, in particular in central and eastern Europe (in some countries, e.g., the then Soviet Union, abortion was used instead of contraception for decades). Abstinence is generally not the answer: In the United States, programmes in favour of abstinence have led to a sharp increase in sexually transmissible diseases, unwanted pregnancies and unavoidable abortions. Facilitating access to emergency contraception at an affordable price and lifting the restriction on over-the-counter sales will also contribute significantly to avoiding abortions.

Making methods of contraception available, however, is not enough to prevent abortions. A recent study in France, which has the highest contraception rate in the world, provided a reminder that almost two of every three unplanned pregnancies occurred in women who claimed to be using a means of contraception when they fell pregnant. It is therefore important to enable women to choose a contraception of suitable nature for them, and chosen by them, to avoid unwanted pregnancies.

Where abortion is legal, safe and accessible in Europe, abortion rates tend to be low.

Banning abortions does not avoid unwanted pregnancies either. Women in a "pregnancy-conflict" can only rarely be persuaded to carry the pregnancy to term against their will—most will seek an abortion even if abortion is illegal in their country. Some will travel to other countries (from Ireland to the United Kingdom, for example). But others, who cannot afford this "abortion tourism", will resort to unsafe "backstreet" abortions or will even try to terminate their pregnancies themselves, at great risk to their health and even life.

Restrictive legislation may also lead to the development of "parallel markets". Some NGOs [nongovernmental organizations] in Poland, where abortion is allowed only in the event of rape, incest or danger to the life or health of the mother, have complained about both women's limited access to abortion and newspaper advertisements publishing such "services".

Ultimately, these associations estimate that some 180,000 clandestine abortions are carried out in Poland every year.

Remove Restrictions

I would thus plead for a more open attitude towards abortion. Where abortion is legal, safe and accessible in Europe, abortion rates tend to be low (also, probably, because most of the countries which take this stance also invest heavily in sex education and accessible contraception). Restrictions on abortion—such as compulsory waiting or "cooling off" periods, requirements for prior consultations or "counselling", or consent by two doctors—are also, in general, counterproductive: as Mr [Christian] Fiala (President of the International Federation of Professional Abortion and Contraception Associates, Austria) pointed out during the hearing, restrictions do not reduce the number of unwanted pregnancies or abortions and do not lead to an increase in the number of women actually having children, nor do they bring about improvements in care: "They merely increase the age of the fetuses [fetuses] at the time of the abortions, with all the related physical and psychological consequences for the mothers. They increase both the physical and psychological health risks and the cost of the operation to no obvious benefit." Furthermore, the more quickly a woman makes her decision, the greater the possibility of abortion through medication being made available to her, thereby avoiding the risks inherent in all surgery.

Finally, it is my personal view that the ultimate decision on whether or not to abort has to be a matter for the woman, and that women's rights to control their own bodies must be recognised.

Jamaica Should Rewrite Its Outdated Abortion Laws

Zadie Neufville

Zadie Neufville is a journalist, writer, and illustrator, and an information technologist with the Caribbean Disaster Emergency Response Agency. In the following viewpoint, she reports that abortion is illegal in most circumstances in Jamaica. As a result, Neufville says, the poor in Jamaica have little access to safe, legal abortions, and many of them resort to dangerous illegal abortions. Neufville concludes that the legislature is considering changing the antiquated laws that contribute to this situation.

As you read, consider the following questions:

1. Under what kind of law are some abortions legal in Jamaica?
2. What does Lana Finikin feel is left out of the debate about abortion in Jamaica?
3. What is the organization DAWN and what is its mission?

When a Jamaican women's group Sistren [Theatre Collective] realised the voices of poor women were missing in a national debate on abortion rights, they boldly staged a play before parliamentarians reviewing a draft law that seeks to clarify when abortion can be deemed legal.

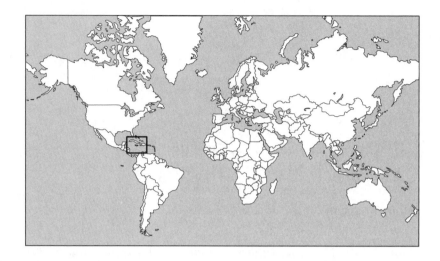

Called *Slice of Reality*, the performance was aimed to give "a voice to groups of women whose experiences may not otherwise be heard", says Lana Finikin, Sistren's executive director. It tells the stories of "poor women who are being robbed of the right to make decisions concerning their own bodies" she told IPS [Inter Press Service] in an interview.

Life Imprisonment for Abortion

The right to abortion is outlawed in Jamaica under an archaic Offences Against the Person Act, which is modeled along the lines of an English law of the same name, legislated in 1861. It prescribes life imprisonment for a woman who aborts her foetus [fetus] and up to three years in jail for the doctor who helps her.

The common law [that is, customary unwritten law based on precedent] under which abortions may be legally carried out, women's activists say, perpetuates a situation where only the rich are able to take advantage. Abortions are allowed in cases of rape, incest, and extreme abnormality of the foetus or danger to the mother, but the only hospital that provided the service to the poor closed in the mid-90s.

Sistren's taut, 10-minute performance on Mar. 12 [2009] was one of dozens of presentations before a joint select committee of Parliament reviewing the pending Termination of Pregnancy Act. The new law seeks to clarify when abortions can be termed legal.

Abortions are allowed in cases of rape, incest, and extreme abnormality of the foetus or danger to the mother, but the only hospital that provided the service to the poor closed in the mid-90s.

Poverty a Stigma

In Kingston's tough inner-city communities, an unplanned pregnancy can mean a lifetime of poverty. Abortion which carries a stigma—scorn and social ostracism—is out of the reach of most women. With only a few doctors willing to do the procedure, the cost of a termination is high, starting at 250 dollars, when daily wage workers earn roughly 43 dollars a week.

As a result, according to Finikin, many risk their lives in unsafe abortions or by consuming dangerous herbal concoctions or lethal drug combinations to cause miscarriages. Health Ministry data show that between Mar. 1 and Aug. 31, 2005, there were 641 admissions due to complications from botched abortions at the island's main maternity hospital in Kingston.

For more than a year now, the joint select committee has been hearing pro- and anti-abortion arguments as it seeks to rewrite the draft legislation.

Finikin feels that the debate is confined to the rights of the foetus and the immorality of the act without regard for the reasons why women decide to abort. She is upset that a poor woman who is raped has no choice. "When you tell me that somebody rapes me, that I must walk with that trauma for nine months and then bring it to fruition . . . ," she said, very graphically expressing the pain [of] many women who have to raise a child born out of rape.

Development Alternatives with Women for a New Era (DAWN), a Caribbean women's rights forum, which has been coordinating the campaign for a just abortion law for the poor, issued a statement. "To continue to criminalise abortion puts women's lives at risk, and suggests that the right of the foetus outweighs the right of women to have control over their own body and life," it noted.

The Sistren Theatre Collective . . . has been at the forefront of educating women about their rights for more than 32 years.

Meanwhile, the pro-life lobby has several well-known members of the Christian clergy in its ranks including a well-known playwright, actor and Jesuit priest Father Richard Ho Lung, a longtime advocate for the poor and founder of the Missionaries of the Poor.

They have accused parliamentarians of supporting abortion, "a barbaric and evil" act, in order to secure money for HIV/AIDS programmes from the European Union and the United States, charges which both have denied.

In Kingston's tough inner-city communities, an unplanned pregnancy can mean a lifetime of poverty.

Lobbying for Reproductive Rights

Opposition member of Parliament [MP] Lisa Hanna who is on the joint parliamentary committee told IPS that in her rural north coast constituency of southeastern St. Ann, women and girls who are desperate to end their pregnancies resort to all sorts of life-threatening solutions.

Slice of Reality portrays these and other stories of mentally ill or other challenged women and those without social sup-

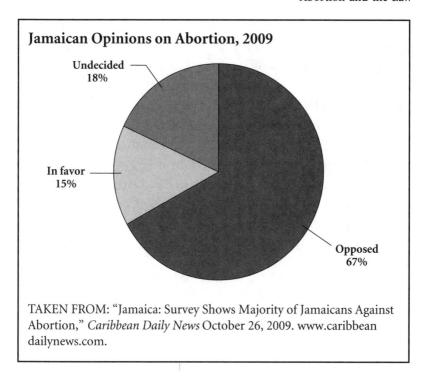

Jamaican Opinions on Abortion, 2009

Undecided
18%

In favor
15%

Opposed
67%

TAKEN FROM: "Jamaica: Survey Shows Majority of Jamaicans Against Abortion," *Caribbean Daily News* October 26, 2009. www.caribbean dailynews.com.

port who are preyed on by abusive men, or girls who are forced into sexual relationships with gunmen in their communities.

Lisa Hanna who is on the joint parliamentary committee told IPS that in her rural north coast constituency . . . women and girls who are desperate to end their pregnancies resort to all sorts of life-threatening solutions.

In addition, there are teenager victims of incestuous relationships who are sworn to secrecy by their families, and women whose husbands refuse to permit them to access birth control methods.

Lobbying for support for women's reproductive rights and (access to) abortion, DAWN states, "it is a woman's right to have all options available to her" so she can make an informed decision.

While the common law allows abortions under specified conditions, it "gives doctors the right over women's lives since not all situations in which women become pregnant, may be strictly in line with the definition provided for under the law", according to DAWN.

With the hearing almost completed, the parliamentary committee will soon make its recommendations.

"All information taken in these hearings will be taken into consideration. The chairman will make our report to Parliament and the legislation will be redrafted," says MP Hanna. She is optimistic that the committee will be able to table the bill in Jamaica's lawmaking lower house of Parliament by year end.

In Jamaica, Abortions Should Remain Illegal

Richard Ho Lung

Richard Ho Lung is a Jamaican Catholic priest who founded Missionaries of the Poor, a monastic order recognized by the Vatican. In the following viewpoint, he argues that the European Union is pushing Jamaica to make abortion easily accessible and to force medical personnel to perform abortions. Ho Lung argues that Europe's atheism and disregard for life will hurt Europe itself as its population ages, and may force Jamaica to become complicit in murder. Ho Lung concludes that Europe should not tie its developmental aid to abortion legalization and should respect Jamaican beliefs.

As you read, consider the following questions:

1. According to Ho Lung, what developing nation had its aid funds cut because of its position on abortion?
2. According to the viewpoint, what pro-abortion groups are funded by Europe and the United Nations?
3. What does the author say will happen in Jamaica if abortion is legalized?

Some pro-abortionists have proposed that in Jamaica, anyone—doctor, nurse, priest, pastor or guidance counsellor—

Richard Ho Lung, "The EU and Abortion," *The Gleaner*, August 3, 2009. Copyright © 2009 Gleaner Company Ltd. Reproduced by permission of the author.

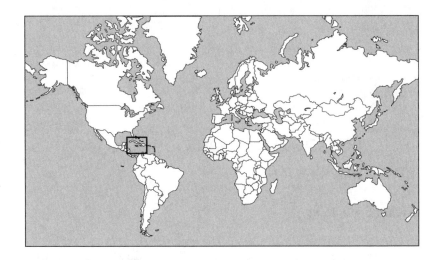

who rejects or advises against abortion should be charged and ofound guilty for not performing or not encouraging the performance of the procedure.

While the proposed bill recommends punishment for medical personnel who do not perform abortions and refuse to advise the woman where she could have one done, at least one pro-abortion group has recommended punishment for persons who speak against abortions in areas where the procedure is done.

Europe Exports Hedonism

We need to understand that abortion is murder. It is the snuffing out of life. Therefore, the new law proposing abortion, and silencing those who are for life, is diabolical. It is a strange reversal of God's law, 'Thou shall not kill'.

The European Union (EU) and its powerful material wealth is often exported along with its hedonism, materialism and atheism so foreign to us. Loans or financial gifts tie us to conditions for some countries in the EU. Abortion is one of those conditions. Let us not forget that nothing is free. I believe there is a new slavery in our times, with the principle that money is king. When we owe money, we are slaves. We must comply with the masters.

In a recent speech (March 2009), Ambassador Marco Mazzocchi-Alemanni of the EU stated that the EU did not tie loans or grants to abortion issues. This is not entirely true. It is known that recently the EU Commissioner [Benita] Ferrero-Waldner had Francesca Mosca as her ambassador threaten the national parliament of Nicaragua to rescind legislation protecting the life of the unborn. Sweden subsequently cut $20 million in aid to that country.

The European Union and its powerful material wealth is often exported along with its hedonism, materialism and atheism so foreign to us.

Also, the German Federal Minister for Economic Cooperation and Development, Heidemarie Wieczorek-Zeul, stated:, "The international community of the donor countries clearly expressed to President Ortega (of Nicaragua) that there will be immediate consequences in terms of development cooperation, if his national piece of legislation is not repealed." Other European countries such as Sweden and Holland seemed to be pushing, if not bullying, other developing countries in matters of abortion.

As atheism, hedonism and materialism replace Judeo-Christian principles of life, Europe seems to be making a death wish. Its population is declining and the graying of Europe seems to be rapidly happening. Nevertheless, it persists in its policy of sex without consequence.

With the event of population growth among the Muslims and their strict moral principles of pro-life, I believe the United Nations (UN) does not dare to enforce abortion explicitly. However, there are agencies receiving tremendous aid for abortion from Europe and from the UN (for example, the UN Population Fund [UNFPA] and the International Planned

Nicaragua's Abortion Ban

Nicaragua's total ban on abortions is endangering the lives of girls and women, denying them lifesaving treatment, preventing health professionals from practicing effective medicine and contributing to an increase in maternal deaths across the country, concludes [the human rights organization] Amnesty International. . . .

The new code introduces criminal sanctions for doctors and nurses who treat a pregnant woman or girl for illnesses such as cancer, malaria, HIV/AIDS or cardiac emergencies where such treatment is contraindicated in pregnancy and may cause injury to or death of the embryo or foetus [fetus].

Amnesty International,
"Shocking Abortion Ban Denies Lifesaving Treatment to Girls
and Women in Nicaragua," July 27, 2009. www.amnesty.org.

Parenthood Federation [IPPF]). This way, the EU promotes abortion but washes its hands clean by passing on the job to other abortion agencies.

I do not want the wombs of our mothers to be the killing fields for innocent babies.

Aid Should Not Interfere with Beliefs

I ask the EU ambassador to Jamaica, Marco Mazzocchi-Alemanni, who disclaims my statement about blood money and abortion: Does the EU promote abortion and tie it to international aid? Does it fund IPPF and the UNFPA which support abortion? Is the EU's help being given in Jamaica for abortion whether it be direct or indirect? What is the relationship with these two agencies in Jamaica?

I wish that the richer countries that have the means would be truly benevolent and be partners in developing our country and other needy countries. We need to develop family life, education, hospitals, housing and agriculture with money that does not interfere with our own way of living and our beliefs.

I do not want the wombs of our mothers to be the killing fields for innocent babies. If abortion is legalised, surely it will become wholesale as has happened in Europe and the United States of America. I do not desire any abortionist to be hurt but to understand the terrible sin committed.

In Queensland, Australia, Legal Confusion over Abortion Must Be Addressed

Caroline de Costa and Michael Carrette

Caroline de Costa and Michael Carrette are medical practitioners who have offered abortion services to women in Far North Queensland, Australia. In the following viewpoint, the authors explain that a woman in Queensland has been prosecuted for taking an oral abortion pill. The prosecution took place under an old Queensland law that is rarely, if ever, enforced. The authors argue that the archaic laws should be quickly changed to protect women and doctors, to conform to practice in the rest of Australia, and to conform to the opinions of most residents of Queensland.

As you read, consider the following questions:

1. According to the authors, of what kind is the vast majority of abortions performed in public hospitals?

2. What kinds of responses do the authors say they have received from the government regarding their concerns about Queensland's abortion laws?

3. According to the authors, when have sections 224, 225, and 226 of the criminal code pertaining to abortion been used historically?

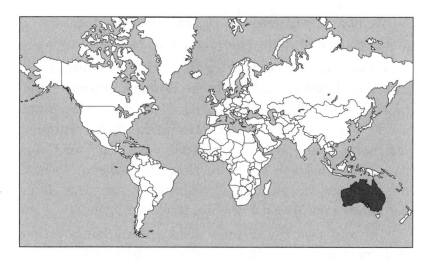

As senior medical practitioners who for the past three years have been offering medical abortion services to women in Far North Queensland, it is with great regret that we announce that we are, at least temporarily, ceasing this practice.

We have decided to cease offering mifepristone(RU-486)/misoprostol [a drug that can be taken orally to cause an abortion in the first two months of pregnancy] early abortion to women in Cairns and surrounding areas.

Prosecution Endangers Patients

This decision has been taken out of concern at the prosecution of a young Cairns woman and her partner under sections 225 and 226 of the Queensland Criminal Code. The implications of this prosecution for us—but more especially the implications for our patients and their support persons—and the complete failure of the Queensland attorney-general and the premier and her government to respond adequately to our communications on this matter.

We are also concerned at the implications for other medical practitioners and nursing staff performing medical abortions in Queensland, and for women undergoing these procedures.

We note that Queensland Health states that medical abortion is performed in the following public hospitals:

Biloela Hospital, Bundaberg Hospital, Caboolture Hospital, Cairns Base Hospital, Gladstone Hospital, Redcliffe Hospital, Gold Coast Hospital, Hervey Bay Hospital, Ipswich Hospital, Kingaroy Hospital, Logan Hospital, Mackay Hospital, Maryborough Hospital, Mount Isa Hospital, Nambour Hospital, Queen Elizabeth II Jubilee Hospital, Redland Hospital, Rockhampton Hospital, Royal Brisbane and Women's Hospital, Toowoomba Hospital and Townsville Hospital. . . .

The vast majority of these abortions are late abortions performed for serious fetal abnormality detected by publicly offered screening services for pregnant women. A few are performed for severe maternal illness. Late medical abortion for fetal abnormality or severe maternal conditions is also performed in a large number of private hospitals in Queensland.

These late abortions are all medical abortions performed using misoprostol, the drug the Cairns woman is currently charged with using to procure an abortion for herself.

Misoprostol is not registered by the Therapeutic Goods Administration (TGA) for the purpose of abortion in Australia so its use in Queensland hospitals, by us, and by many other practitioners in other states, is "off-label"—a widespread and accepted practice among medical professionals.

Abortion Increases Options for Women

In April 2006 we were granted permission by the TGA to use mifepristone (RU-486) together with misoprostol for early abortion in Cairns, for women with "life-threatening or otherwise serious conditions" that would be exacerbated by continuing pregnancy. We have safely and successfully used the drugs in such cases for the past three years.

In all our cases women have first undergone counseling with discussion of the alternatives to abortion, have had appropriate medical examinations and have been appropriately supported through the abortion and follow-up procedures.

We believe that medical abortion had greatly increased the options open to women in the Cairns region who have had to make the difficult decision about abortion for themselves.

We have not witnessed anything in our practice during this time that would suggest that the provision of medical abortion itself is influencing a woman's decision to terminate a pregnancy; we are simply aware that the options for women have increased. Our practice of RU-486/misoprostol abortion has been closely overseen by the TGA to whom we report twice yearly.

We believe that medical abortion had greatly increased the options open to women in the Cairns region who have had to make the difficult decision about abortion for themselves.

Nevertheless throughout the past three years we have been very aware of the anomalies in Queensland law with regard to the practice of medical abortion, and indeed the practice of abortion where the indication is severe fetal abnormality.

We have, individually and together, frequently expressed our concerns in writing and in speaking publicly to the media and to our professional colleagues. We, and others, have addressed numerous letters to the previous and current premier and government ministers, and to the Queensland branch of the Australian Medical Association (AMA).

Despite our legitimate concerns and our status as members of the medical profession we have received (usually) no response whatever; where there have been responses these have been curt brush-offs from junior bureaucrats, or stock answers such as abortion is "a divisive issue" or "a matter for a woman and her doctor."

Australia's Abortion Gag

Not only does Australia refuse to train doctors [who receive Australian government aid in developing countries] in the provision of safe abortions, we won't provide funds to any groups or organisations that dare to give women *information* on abortions. . . .

This is despite the fact that abortion is freely available to women in our own country. . . . The only message one can take from this is that the Australian government believes women in poor and developing countries are not entitled to the same rights as Australian women.

Ruby Murray,
"Australia's Abortion Gag," Newmatilda.com,
January 27, 2009. http://newmatilda.com.

The Criminal Code Makes Abortion a Crime

Queensland abortion law is contained within the Queensland Criminal Code in sections 224–226. Section 224 states that a doctor who performs an abortion commits a crime, section 225 that a woman procuring an abortion commits a crime, and section 226 that anyone providing substance or thing to aid the abortion commits a crime. There are substantial terms of imprisonment attached to these sections.

There is a defence for the person charged with one or more of these crimes in section 282 of the Code—which allows a "surgical operation" for the preservation of the mother's life if the performance of the operation is reasonable. (The term "surgical operation" appears only in the Queensland Code; abortion remains a crime in some other Australian states, but the defence is not restricted to surgical procedures.)

Section 282 was broadly interpreted in the case of Dr Peter Bayliss and Dr Dawn Cullen in 1986. These two doctors were acquitted on charges of procuring an abortion, and the judgment from that case, the *McGuire* judgment, is the case law on which doctors currently performing abortions in Queensland would rely if similarly charged.

Section 224 states that a doctor who performs an abortion commits a crime, section 225 that a woman procuring an abortion commits a crime, and section 226 that anyone providing any substance or thing to aid the abortion commits a crime.

The Queensland Criminal Code dates from 1899, and was in turn based upon the English Offences Against the Person Act of 1861, using, in the sections dealing with abortion, virtually the same wording. Section 224 of the Code has been used very rarely since 1899. Section 225 was used in 1955 (probably the only occasion on which it has been used); the woman concerned was convicted in a lower court, but the conviction was overturned on appeal. Section 226 has probably never been used, and certainly not in the last 50 years.

At the time the Queensland Criminal Code was introduced, safe abortion using drugs (i.e., medical abortion) was completely unknown.

Change the Law

The law was originally designed to protect women from unsafe backstreet abortions—it failed to do this at the time it was promulgated and it is completely at odds with the contemporary practice of abortion and the views of the majority of Australians who believe that safe legal abortion should be accessible to all women.

The fact that a woman and her partner have been charged in Cairns under sections 225 and 226 of the Code is a personal tragedy for these two young people, but it also carries major implications for our practice of medical abortion.

While we appreciate that no Australian medical professional appears to have been involved in the case currently before the courts, we had been over the past three years assured privately by politicians and members of the police that no prosecutions would ever be made under sections 224–226, unless a woman was seriously harmed or died, neither of which events appear to have occurred in this case.

The law was originally designed to protect women from unsafe backstreet abortions—it failed to do this at the time it was promulgated and it is completely at odds with the contemporary practice of abortion.

We are also aware, from media reports, that there was a period of three months between the date of the alleged offence and the reporting of the matter to the police. Nothing is known to us of who made this report, but it appears that the person or persons may have been highly motivated to bring about the public shaming and possible conviction of these people—who have apparently done nothing more than use a drug widely available to women for the purpose of abortion elsewhere in Australia and overseas. We are concerned that one of our patients might be the next target.

We have therefore jointly sought legal advice, initially from a solicitor [a lawyer who deals with legal matters other than trial advocacy]. This lawyer has briefed a barrister [a lawyer who argues cases in trial] with expertise in criminal law and we await that person's professional opinion on our position, and even more critically for us, on the position of our patients and their support persons. As medical practitioners we place the highest importance on the physical and emotional well-being and safety of our patients. The initial legal advice we have received has led us to our current course of action.

We would also recommend that all our medical colleagues in Queensland currently practising or assisting with medical abortion likewise consider their legal position and that of their patients.

We will also be continuing our efforts to communicate with the Queensland government and the Queensland AMA executive. It is unfortunate that there has so far been no recognition on the part of these elected bodies that this issue is not about the ethics or morality of abortion, and no understanding that the personal opinions of elected officials should not form the basis for response to legitimate public concerns.

This issue is about the current impediments to the safe and accessible provision for Queensland women of services that are much more freely and legally available elsewhere in Australia.

We would like to see the premier send the existing archaic abortion law to the Queensland Law Reform Commission, for recommendations for updating abortion regulations that can then be considered and voted upon in Parliament. This has happened successfully in Victoria [another Australian state]; it should also be possible in Queensland.

In Queensland, Australia, Abortion Laws Need Not Be Changed

Paul Dobbyn

Paul Dobbyn is a journalist with the Catholic Leader, *a Catholic newspaper in Brisbane, Australia. In the following viewpoint, he talks to pro-life advocates who insist that although the Queensland law against abortion is rarely enforced, it reflects opinion in Queensland and serves a valuable moral function. The viewpoint also argues that the law protects women against pressures to abort their children. Therefore, Dobbyn asserts, the law should not be altered, and in fact, there should be more restrictions on distributing abortion pills. In addition, Dobbyn's interviewees say there should be more grassroots efforts to aid women who want to keep their babies.*

As you read, consider the following questions:

1. According to Teresa Martin, how many women in Queensland have abortions each year, and what does this show about the difficulty of obtaining abortions there?

2. According to Teresa Martin, the laws against abortion protect women against pressure from whom?

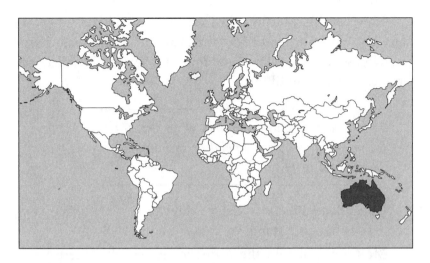

3. According to Bishop Morris, why does Marie Stopes International have a conflict of interest when it distributes RU-486?

A claim that Queensland faced "a legal medical emergency" which would open the door for the state to follow last year's [2008's] lead from Victoria and decriminalise abortion was ridiculous, Cherish Life Queensland (CLQ) president Teresa Martin said last week [August 2009].

Queensland Opposes Abortion

In a story in the *Australian*, former state Labor MP [Member of Parliament] Bonny Barry made the claim after the prosecution of a Cairns couple for illegally importing the abortion drug RU-486 and then using it without medical supervision to procure the abortion of their unborn child.

Ms Barry, in what was seen as an attempt to put pressure on Premier Anna Bligh to act, also revealed that draft legislation dating back to 2003 existed to decriminalise abortion in Queensland.

However, Ms Martin called on Queensland parliamentarians "to stand firm and reject the brutal laws that Victoria recently passed, under which any unborn baby can be killed, for any reason at all until birth".

---

53 per cent of Queenslanders were opposed to abortion for non-medical, or financial or social reasons, with only 28 per cent in favour.

Queensland Bioethics Centre director Ray Campbell supported Ms Martin's stand.

Mr Campbell told the *Catholic Leader* that "there is no doubt that pro-abortion groups are using the unfortunate case in northern Queensland as an excuse to once again push for a change to the abortion law in Queensland", adding that "the case itself is very curious".

Ms Martin said recent research showed 53 per cent of Queenslanders were opposed to abortion for non-medical, or financial or social reasons, with only 28 per cent in favour.

She said Ms Barry was indulging in wishful thinking if she thought the people of Queensland would support such a depraved law.

"Where is this so-called 'legal medical emergency'?" Ms Martin said. "The fact that 15,000 Queensland women have abortions each year shows that unfortunately there is no difficulty in obtaining an abortion in this state.

"Even though not often enforced, the law against abortion still has a vital educative role, instructing society that the intentional killing of pre-born humans is totally wrong.

"The law against abortion also needs to remain on the statute books as a safeguard for women against being pressured by their partners and an essential defence for doctors and nurses who refuse to cooperate in the killing of unborn children."

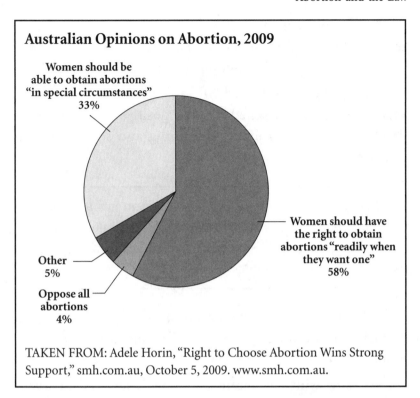

Australian Opinions on Abortion, 2009

Women should be able to obtain abortions "in special circumstances" 33%

Women should have the right to obtain abortions "readily when they want one" 58%

Other 5%

Oppose all abortions 4%

TAKEN FROM: Adele Horin, "Right to Choose Abortion Wins Strong Support," smh.com.au, October 5, 2009. www.smh.com.au.

Mr Campbell said it was "very sad that the best support that some people are able to offer a woman who is pregnant and is worried about carrying on with the pregnancy is to offer them a pill to take so as to kill their baby".

Victoria's Legislation Is No Solution

"Pro-abortion advocates continually hail the new legislation in Victoria as a model, and yet this piece of legislation offered next to nothing by way of support to women who are struggling with their pregnancy," he said.

"The only answer the Victorian government has to a difficult situation is to make it easier to kill the baby while at the same time seeking to punish those who want to help both the woman and her baby.

"It is good that many groups are already campaigning to let their local politicians know that they do not favour any further loosening of the laws on abortion in Queensland".

Mr Campbell also noted "the archdiocese of Brisbane [in Queensland] has launched its own positive response to the needs of women through establishing and supporting the Walking with Love campaign".

The only answer the Victorian government has to a difficult situation is to make it easier to kill the baby while at the same time seeking to punish those who want to help both the woman and her baby.

"This is a grassroots campaign of people who are willing to make themselves available to assist women who are pregnant," he said.

"Walking with Love groups are now established in several parishes and more parishes are expressing interest."

Another Brisbane group Pregnancy Crisis Inc has recently assisted several women who chose to have their babies rather than abort them.

Meanwhile, Bishop [William] Morris expressed "grave concerns for the health and well-being of women" given that RU-486 would now be made more readily available from Marie Stopes International [an international nongovernmental organization that works on sexual and reproductive health issues].

"I do have grave concerns for women seeking out the services of Marie Stopes International now that the organisation has been granted approval by the Therapeutic Goods Administration [an Australian government agency] to administer RU-486 which in effect triggers a miscarriage with the popping of a pill," he said.

"Effectively this means that an agency that receives a financial compensation for the provision of the abortion is the same one providing the advice—which is a clear conflict of interest.

"It is extremely troubling to me that it appears that Marie Stopes International will in effect be able to administer RU-486 at the request of a sometimes confused, troubled, distressed patient without having to meet requirements that exist for other authorised prescribers of the drug."

Bishop Morris said it was well known that the Catholic Church sought to protect human life in all situations—including life in the womb.

"Women faced with an unwanted or unplanned pregnancy are often confronted with one of the most challenging of life situations," he said.

"Ensuring that women have access to the full range of care and support options at this time is critical."

Bishop Morris said church agencies such as Centacare provided pregnancy support services for any woman facing an unplanned pregnancy.

Periodical Bibliography

The following articles have been selected to supplement the diverse views presented in this chapter.

N.C. Aizenman   "Nicaragua's Total Ban on Abortion Spurs Critics," *Washington Post*, November 28, 2006. www.washingtonpost.com.

BBC News   "Europe's Abortion Rules," February 12, 2007. http://news.bbc.co.uk.

Carmel Crimmins   "Abortion in the Philippines: A National Secret," Reuters, September 5, 2007. www.reuters .com.

Cicely Gosier   "Ireland's Abortion Law Gets Help from U.S.," CBN.com, September 23, 2008. www.cbn.com.

Lindy Kerin   "Queensland Abortion Trial 'Will Increase Anxiety,'" ABC News, September 11, 2009. www.abc.net.au.

Marianne Mollman   "Abortion Lessons from Latin America," Human Rights Watch, March 21, 2006. www.hrw.org.

Kathy Newman   "Bligh Is a Hypocrite on Queensland Abortion Law," *Punch*, September 28, 2009. www.thepunch.com.au.

Pew Forum on   "Abortion Laws Around the World," September
Religion & Public Life 30, 2008. http://pewforum.org.

Elisabeth Rosenthal "Legal or Not, Abortion Rates Compare," *New York Times*, October 12, 2007. www .nytimes.com.

Danielle Toppin   "Jamaica's Flawed Abortion Laws," RH Reality Check, March 28, 2008. www.rhreality check.org.

GLOBALVIEWPOINTS

Abortion and Sex Selection

Worldwide, Selective Abortions Cause Shortage of Women

Joan Delaney

Joan Delaney is a Canadian staff writer for the Epoch Times, *a newspaper based in New York. In the following viewpoint, she notes that in many countries such as China and India, families that want sons check gender with ultrasounds and then abort female fetuses. Delaney says that this practice is causing gender imbalances, resulting in social unrest and trafficking in brides. Delaney writes that the Canadian government has opposed international efforts to restrict the practice on pro-choice grounds. Delaney suggests that this opposition should end and more should be done to restrict sex-selective abortion for both moral and social reasons.*

As you read, consider the following questions:

1. What is the sex ratio in India, according to Delaney?
2. According to Joseph D'Agostino, what percentage of China's orphans are girls?
3. In addition to Asian countries, where does Delaney say that sex-selective abortion is common?

Boy or girl? Pink or blue? Gender selection has historically existed in some form or another in many cultures, but thanks to technological advances in recent years, it has become an accepted and widespread practice in a number of developing countries.

Ultrasound and Abortion

The availability of cheap ultrasound scans in Asian countries within the last 20 years has made it possible for even the poorest woman to discern the sex of her unborn child.

Sex selection in countries such as China and India is now achieved mainly through ultrasound, followed by an abortion if the fetus is female. While the natural sex ratio is about 105 boys per 100 girls, in India it has climbed to 113 boys per 100 girls, and up to 156 boys per 100 girls in some regions.

The current sex ratio in China is about 120 boys per 100 girls, and in the more prosperous provinces it's even higher. Although both countries have banned sex-selective abortion, India back in 1994 and China more recently, it is still widely practised.

Sex selection in countries such as China and India is now achieved mainly through ultrasound, followed by an abortion if the fetus is female.

The reasons for the high abortion rates of girls are many and varied. Both India and China, as well as other countries that use sex-selective abortions widely, have a long-standing preference for boys, especially in rural areas. It often comes down to practicalities: A son can work the farm, carry on the family name, and look after elderly parents, whereas a daughter will become part of her husband's family after she gets married.

In India, where the cost of a dowry for a daughter can be prohibitive, financial pressure is often a reason for resorting to sex-selective abortion or infanticide. A 2006 study published in the British medical journal, the *Lancet*, estimated that up to half a million female fetuses are aborted every year in India.

But China's strict one-child policy [which legally restricts couples to one child], implemented in 1979 to reduce the population, has severely upset the gender balance in that country. A January report in the *China Daily* estimated that there will be 30 million more men than women of marriageable age in China by 2020, leading to possible widespread social unrest.

Sex Selection Leads to Social Problems

Already, the skewed sex ratio has resulted in a rise in the kidnapping and trafficking of women, both within the country and internationally. Mail order bride services have mushroomed, which, for a fee of up to $2,400, import wives for Chinese men from other countries, especially Burma. Joseph D'Agostino, vice president for communications with the Virginia-based Population Research Institute (PRI), calls the one-child policy "a massive violation of human rights" which affects both women and men.

"When it comes to sex-selective abortion, it's something that's leading to grave social problems—the extermination of tens of millions of girls," says D'Agostino. "And of course it's bad for the boys too because they're going to grow up and not be able to get married. It seems to be against everyone's interests except the very elite and the Communist government that runs China, which has its own agenda and its own goals."

> *Already the skewed sex ratio has resulted in a rise in the kidnapping and trafficking of women, both within the country [China] and internationally.*

D'Agostino says Beijing has now become aware of the problems of sex selection, and recently introduced cash bonuses for families who have girls, but the gap in the boy/girl ratio is still widening. Meanwhile, the one-child policy will remain firmly in place for another 50 years, the goal being to reduce China's population from the present 1.2 billion to 600 million.

Because of the policy, pregnant women are subjected to harassment, financial penalties, and forced abortions and sterilization, often in the late stages of pregnancy. Chen Guangcheng, a blind activist who has fought against the one-child policy, said last October [2006] that more than 120,000 women in Shandong province alone were at that time forced to undergo sterilizations and abortions. Forced abortion and sterilization is enforced in Tibet as well.

The Dying Rooms, a shocking British documentary that created an outcry around the world, showed children abandoned in some of China's state orphanages, uncared for and left to die in unimaginable misery and squalour, victims of the one-child policy. D'Agostino says 95 percent of China's orphans are girls.

In 2005, a U.N. [United Nations] report stated that the number of "missing" girls resulting from abortion and female infanticide is now at an estimated 200 million worldwide. In an effort to combat the problem, the United States last week [March 2007] sponsored a resolution at the U.N.'s Commission on the Status of Women calling on states to eliminate infanticide and gender selection.

But the resolution was withdrawn, thanks to opposition from China, India, Mexico and other countries—one of which apparently was Canada. Mary Ellen Douglas, national organizer with the Campaign Life Coalition which had a representative present at the two-week conference, said the resolution contained language that the Canadian delegation didn't agree with, and so they maneuvered against it. ·

"The Canadians are constantly trying to get the language of women's rights into everything, and they claim that they're

Sex-Selective Abortions in Canada

[Sex-selective abortion] made headlines in August [2007] because of a protest in Surrey, BC [British Columbia] against advertisements placed in South Asian–targeted newspapers. The ads were paid for by an American private ultrasound clinic owner, Dr John Stephens, who was offering sex-determination testing to BC's Indian community. Local community activists accuse him of providing scans at 12 weeks to parents who go on to terminate female fetuses.

Sam Solomon,
"Sex-Selective Abortion Comes to Canada,"
National Review of Medicine, *September 15, 2007.*
www.nationalreviewofmedicine.com.

doing this as a matter of justice. But their goal it seems is to get a universal right to abortion—that's the bottom line for them," says Douglas.

Although the Department of Foreign Affairs says that "Canada did not block the resolution," Samantha Singson [the director of government relations for C-FAM] asserts that, although she didn't attend the closed session, she "got it from sources in the negotiating room that Canada worked very hard to ensure that the resolution would be withdrawn."

Gender Imbalance in Many Nations

Douglas says she was surprised that one of the countries that backed the resolution was South Korea, a country with a strong preference for sons. But maybe it's not so surprising, given that the South Korean government, recognizing that there's a severe gender imbalance in the country because of sex-selective abortions, has been attempting to change public opinion with a "Love Your Daughter" campaign. Meanwhile, South Korean men have been traveling to other countries, primarily Vietnam, to find a wife.

India has been trying to turn the trend around with new laws introduced in 2002 that prohibit the disclosure of the sex of the fetus or advertising services that determine the sex of the fetus. But so far, only one doctor has been charged. Last year, China dropped a proposal to impose fines and prison terms for sex-selective abortion.

A 1993 Royal Commission on New Reproductive Technologies found that 90 per cent of Canadians were uncomfortable with the idea of gender-selective abortions.

As well as in many Asian countries, gender-selective abortions are common in Cuba, Venezuela and Pakistan, and also within immigrant communities in Canada and the United States. A recent *Western Standard* article reported that some Asian immigrants are seeking sex-selective abortions in Canada, and being accommodated by clinics in B.C. [British Columbia] and Ontario. A B.C. clinician interviewed for the story estimated she sees women who want to abort female fetuses at a rate of about one per week.

But sex-selective abortion is not within the realm of acceptance for most Canadians. A 1993 Royal Commission on New Reproductive Technologies found that 90 per cent of Canadians were uncomfortable with the idea of gender-selective abortions.

And although many who are "pro-choice" draw the line at aborting a fetus because of gender preference, the Abortion Rights Coalition of Canada has issued a position paper on sex selection stating, "It is important to remember that we cannot restrict women's right to abortion just because some women might make decisions we disagree with."

One of the latest high-tech sex-selection methods to appear in the United States is a sperm sorting technique which is marketed as a way to achieve "family balancing" or "family completion." Demographers and women's rights groups are concerned that an increased acceptance of gender selection in the United States will serve to exacerbate the problem in countries where "son preference" prevails.

D'Agostino, who believes the gender imbalance "is turning into a huge global problem that's getting worse every year," says his organization would like to see sex-selective abortion outlawed in the United States. He says it should be more prominent on the U.N.'s agenda, and that countries need to work to "change the culture around this and hopefully change the laws."

"There needs to be some sort of global approach to this because it's fast becoming a social problem," says D'Agostino. "It's not only immoral, it's impractical, and people need to have a different mentality."

In China, Selective Abortions Have Created a Gender Imbalance

Wei Xing Zhu, Li Lu, and Therese Hesketh

Wei Xing Zhu is professor of law, political science, and public administration at Zhejiang Normal University in China[1]; Li Lu is professor of social and family medicine at Zhejiang University in China[2]; Therese Hesketh is a professor of international health and development at University College London.[3] In the following viewpoint, they note that in China, legal restrictions on the number of children, preference for male children, and technologies like ultrasound have caused many female fetuses to be aborted. The authors argue that census data indicate that this has resulted in a gender imbalance. They also note that China is attempting to address this problem, and that there is some evidence that the gender imbalance may soon decline.

As you read, consider the following questions:

1. According to the authors, the sex ratio at birth usually slightly favors boys. Why then is the sex ratio usually close to even during the reproductive years?

2. The authors estimate that an excess of how many males were born in the twelve months leading up to October 2005?

Wei Xing Zhu, Li Lu, and Therese Hesketh, "China's Excess Males, Sex Selective Abortion, and One Child Policy: Analysis of Data from 2005 National Intercensus Survey," *BMJ*, April 9, 2009. Copyright © Zhu et al. 2009. Copyright © 2009 British Medical Association. Reproduced by permission.

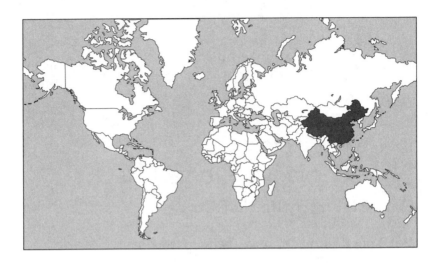

3. What is the type 2 variation of the one-child policy, as described by the authors?

Abstract

Objectives. To elucidate current trends and geographical patterns in the sex ratio at birth and in the population aged under 20 in China and to determine the roles played by sex selective abortion and the one child policy.

Design. Analysis of household based cross sectional population survey done in November 2005.

Setting. All of China's 2861 counties.

Population. 1% of the total population, selected to be broadly representative of the total.

Main outcome measure. Sex ratio defined as males per 100 females.

Results. 4 764 512 people under the age of 20 were included. Overall sex ratios were high across all age groups and residency types, but they were highest in the 1–4 years age group, peaking at 126 (95% confidence interval 125 to 126) in rural areas. Six provinces had sex ratios of over 130 in the 1–4 age group. The sex ratio at birth was close to normal for first order births but rose steeply for second order births, especially in rural areas, where it reached 146 (143 to 149). Nine provinces had ratios of over 160 for second order births. The highest sex ratios were seen in provinces that allow rural inhabitants a second child if the first is a girl. Sex selective abortion accounts for almost all the excess males. One particular variant of the one child policy, which allows a second child if the first is a girl, leads to the highest sex ratios.

Conclusions. In 2005 males under the age of 20 exceeded females by more than 32 million in China, and more than 1.1 million excess births of boys occurred. China will see very high and steadily worsening sex ratios in the reproductive age group over the next two decades. Enforcing the existing ban on sex selective abortion could lead to normalisation of the ratios.

Introduction

In the absence of intervention, the sex ratio at birth is consistent across populations at between 103 and 107 boys born for every 100 girls.[1,2] Higher early mortality among boys ensures a ratio of close to 100 in the all important reproductive years. However, in many countries, mainly in South and East Asia, the sex ratio deviates from this norm because of the tradition of preference for sons.[3] Historically, preference for sons has been manifest postnatally through female infanticide and the neglect and abandonment of girls.[4] Where this persists, it mainly consists of failure to access necessary medical care.[5,6] However, since the early 1980s selection for males prenatally with ultrasonographic sex determination and sex selective abortion has been possible. This technology has become widely available in many countries, leading to high sex ratios from birth.[5] The highest sex ratios are seen in countries with a combination of preference for sons, easy access to sex selective technology, and a low fertility rate, as births of girls must be prevented to allow for the desired number of sons within the family size.[7] In the era of the one child policy the fact that the problem of excess males in China seems to outstrip that of all other countries is perhaps no surprise.[6,8]

Some of the evidence for this sex imbalance in China has been challenged, because accurate population based figures have been difficult to obtain.[9,10] Births classified as "illegal," violating the one child policy, may be concealed to avoid penalties.[11,12] Underreporting of births of girls may be more common in this context, leading to spuriously high sex ratios at birth.[13,14] However, if girls are not reported at birth, they are likely to filter into the statistics later, as registration is necessary for immunisation or to start school.[15] Therefore, examining the sex ratio across different age bands provides a more accurate picture.

The objectives of this study were to elucidate current trends and geographical patterns in the sex ratio at birth and in the population under the age of 20 in China and to explore the role played by sex selective abortion and the one child policy in the sex imbalance.

Methods

We analysed data from the intercensus survey of 2005, which was carried out on a representative 1% of the total population in November 2005 and is the most recent national population survey. It used the same basic organisation, procedures, and questionnaire as the fifth census of 2000, but the mode of implementation took into account acknowledged deficiencies of the 2000 census, which led to under-numeration of the population by an estimated 1.8%, mostly in the youngest age groups, resulting in possible inaccuracies in the sex ratio.[16] Specific measures were therefore incorporated into this survey to solve problems of under-numeration, and quality control methods were used to minimise sampling bias. These are described in detail elsewhere.[16] The survey covered all of China's 2861 counties, using a three stage cluster sampling method at township, village, and enumeration district level, with probability proportionate to estimated size, and is hence broadly representative of the total population. The minimal sampling unit was the enumeration district, which consisted of the village committee in rural areas and the neighbourhood committee in urban areas. The survey was carried out in households by staff specifically trained in census techniques. Only data for the under 20 age group are reported here.

Analysis—The major outcome variable is the sex ratio, defined as males per 100 females. We derived 95% confidence intervals for the sex ratios by using the 95% confidence interval for the proportion of female births (pf) with a variance of pf(1-pf). We calculated the excess of males for all age groups by using an average of the mean sex ratios from 13 countries that have normal secondary sex ratios and little or no sex preference.[17] These were 105 for the 1–9 age group and 104 for the 10–19 age group.

Results

The survey counted 4 764 512 people under the age of 20: 1 073 229 (22%) urban residents, 813 386 (17%) town residents, and 2 877 897 (60%) rural inhabitants. In the 12 months before the study 161 109 births were reported: 23% in urban areas, 17% in towns, and 60% in rural areas. First order births accounted for 63% of the total, second order for 32%, third order for 4.3%, and fourth or higher order for 1%.

Under 20 sex ratio. Table 1 [shown in "Sex Ratios in China, 2005" in this viewpoint] shows the sex ratio by age group and type of residency. Sex ratios were consistently higher than normal across residency type and all age groups except for urban 15–19 year olds. Sex ratios peaked in the 1–4 age group; the highest was 126 (95% confidence interval 125 to 126) in

Sex Ratios in China, 2005

The table shows the ratio of boys to 100 girls. So, for example, it shows that for all children under 1 year, the sex ratio was 119 boys to 100 girls.

	Under 1 year	1–4 years	5–9 years	10–14 years	15–19 years
All	119	124	119	114	108
Urban	114	116	116	112	101
Town	117	122	121	116	109
Rural	122	126	120	114	111

TAKEN FROM: Wei Xing Zhu, Li Liu, and Therese Hesketh, "China's Excess Males, Sex Selective Abortion, and One Child Policy: Analysis of Data from 2005 National Intercensus Survey," *BMJ,* vol. 338, April 9, 2009. www.bmj.com.

rural areas. Table 2 [not shown] shows the sex ratio by age group for all provinces. Only two provinces, Tibet and Xinjiang, had sex ratios within normal limits across the age range. Two provinces, Jiangxi and Henan, had ratios of over 140 in the 1–4 age group; four provinces—Anhui, Guangdong, Hunan, and Hainan—had ratios of over 130; and seven provinces had ratios between 120 and 129. The provinces with the highest sex ratios are clustered together in the central-southern region (fig. 1 [not shown]). Notably, sex ratios were high into the teenage groups in Hainan and Guangxi. The excess of males increased from 5.1% (n=142 634) in the cohort born between 1986 and 1995 to 9.4% (n=184 970) in the cohort born between 1996 and 2005 across the whole country. A marked rise occurred in the percentage of excess males between the two cohorts in all provinces except Xinjiang.

Sex ratio at birth. The total sex ratio at birth for the 12 months to October 2005 was 120 (119 to 121) for the whole sample (table 3 [not shown]), with a gradient between urban

(115, 113 to 117), town (120, 118 to 122), and rural (123, 121 to 124) areas. This equates to 11 320 excess boys born for the year for the whole sample. The total sex ratio at birth was over 130 in three provinces (Shaanxi, Anhui, and Jiangxi) and over 120 in 14 provinces. These overall figures conceal dramatic differences in sex ratio at birth by birth order. The sex ratio at birth for first order births was slightly high in cities and towns but was within normal limits in rural areas. However, the ratio rose very steeply for second and higher order births in cities 138 (132 to 144), towns 137 (131 to 143), and rural areas 146 (143 to 149), although the numbers of second order births in cities were low. These rises were consistent across all provinces, except Tibet, with very high figures for second births in Anhui (190, 176 to 205) and Jiangsu (192, 174 to 212). For third births, the sex ratio rose to over 200 in four provinces, although third births accounted for only 4.3% of the total.

Discussion

The findings paint a discouraging picture of very high and increasing sex ratios in the reproductive age group in China for the next two decades. The sex ratio increased steadily from 108 (108 to 109) in the cohort born between 1985 and 1989 to 124 (123 to 124) in the 2000 to 2004 cohort. However, the ratio then declined to 119 (119 to 120) for the 2005 cohort, perhaps indicating the beginning of a reduction in sex ratios for the future. Sex ratios were outside the normal range for almost all age groups in almost all provinces. The sex ratios rose dramatically between first and second order births, with very high sex ratios for the very few higher order births. Tibet and Xinjiang were the notable exceptions. The highest ratios were seen in the centre and south of the country, in the highly populous provinces of Henan, Jiangxi, Anhui, Guangdong, and Hainan. Extrapolating from this 1% sample to the whole country, we estimate that an excess of 1 132 000 boys were born in the 12 months to October 2005 and that an excess of 32 706 400 males under the age of 20 existed in the whole of China at that time, 18 497 000 of them under the age of 10.

This is the most recent nationwide demographic survey in China, a country undergoing rapid socioeconomic change, where timely data are of particular importance. The survey used specific measures to attempt to ensure coverage of the target group, in order to more accurately estimate the sex ratio.[16] A very large survey aiming to represent 1% of the total population obviously has some limitations. Complete coverage of households and inhabitants is clearly impossible on such a large scale. Furthermore, extrapolation to the whole population from a 1% sample should be done with caution. The small sample size at provincial level in some age bands and for second and higher order births leads to wide confidence intervals, illustrating the uncertainty around these figures. However, the overall credibility of the data is increased by the high sex ratios in older age groups, for which concealment and underreporting of girls would be difficult, and by the number of births counted for the 12 months to October 2005 (161 109), which matches the estimate of 16 million births a year from other sources.[18] The findings increase our understanding of the roles of sex selective abortion and the influence of the one child policy in the sex imbalance in China and have clear policy implications.

The findings paint a discouraging picture of very high and increasing sex ratios in the reproductive age group in China for the next two decades.

Role of Sex Selective Abortion. The precise role of sex selective abortion in the sex imbalance has been unclear, not least because the practice is illegal in China and obtaining reliable figures is therefore difficult. Some small rural studies have made estimates for proportions of sex selective abortions from hospital based and community birth records.[19,20,21] Two concluded that sex selective abortion was the major cause of the sex imbalance; however, local circumstances vary hugely in China, so wider inferences need to be made with caution. The findings of this survey help to elucidate the role of sex selective abortion in the high sex ratio at the national level.

Although sex selective abortion is illegal, proving that an abortion has been carried out on sex selective as opposed to family planning grounds is often difficult when abortion itself is so readily available.

Firstly, if under-registration of girls, rather than sex selective abortion, accounted for most of the excess births of boys, then sex ratios would fall from birth through early childhood, as girls are required to be registered for immunisation and school entry.[15] Our finding that the sex ratios for the 1–4-year-old cohort are higher than those at birth and in infancy tends to refute this hypothesis, suggesting that the rise in the 1–4 age group is a cohort effect—that is, it reflects the higher sex ratio at birth in this cohort. To further investigate the role of under-registration, comparison can be made between each cohort specific sex ratio and the corresponding sex ratio at birth from previous census data.[22,23] This shows that with only one exception, the 15–19-year-old cohort born between 1985 and 1989, the sex ratio at birth was higher or very close to the sex ratio of the corresponding birth cohort in the 2005 survey: The age 1–4 cohort had a sex ratio of 124 and a sex ratio at birth of 120, the 5–9 cohort had a sex ratio of 119 and a sex ratio at birth of 118, the corresponding ratios for the 10–14 cohort were 114 and 112, and those for the 15–19 cohort were 108 and 111. This lends support to the assertion that under-registration of girls is not a major contributor to high sex ratios at birth. Infanticide is of course another possible explanation for girls missing at birth, but this is widely acknowledged to be very rare now.[24,25,26,27]

Secondly, the dramatic increase in sex ratio with second births that our data document, shows that couples are selecting to ensure a boy, the so-called "at least one son practice."[15] In urban areas where few couples are allowed a second child, the high sex ratio for first order births (110, 95% confidence interval 107 to 113) suggests some sex selection occurring with the only child. This pattern of dramatic increases in sex ratios for second children is not unique to China. In both South Korea and parts of India, where overall sex ratios are high, the sex ratio increases dramatically for second and higher order births, which has been attributed to sex selective abortion, as couples try to ensure the birth of male offspring while limiting their family size.[7,28]

Thirdly, the steady rise in sex ratios across the birth cohorts since 1986 mirrors the increasing availability of ultrasonography over that period. The first ultrasound machines were used in the early 1980s; they reached county hospitals by the late 1980s and then rural townships by the mid-1990s.[21,29] Since then, ultrasonography has been very cheap and available even to the rural poor. Termination of pregnancy is also very available, in line with the one child policy.[26] Although sex selective abortion is illegal, proving that an abortion has been carried out on sex selective as opposed to family planning grounds is often difficult when abortion itself is so readily available.[21]

Role of One Child Policy. The relation between the sex ratio and the one child policy is a complex one. This study covers births taking place after the policy was instigated, so the increase in sex ratio that we document across age cohorts born in the past 20 years cannot be blamed on the policy in itself. However, the policy is implemented differently across the country (fig. 2 [not shown]), and our data do suggest that the sex ratio is related to the way in which the policy is implemented.[15] Whereas in most cities only one child is allowed, three main variants of the policy exist in rural areas. Type 1 provinces are most restrictive—around 40% of couples are allowed a second child but generally only if the first is a girl. In type 2 provinces everyone is allowed a second child if the first is a girl or if parents with one child experience "hardship," the definition of which is open to interpretation by local officials. Type 3 provinces are most permissive, allowing couples a second child and sometimes a third, irrespective of sex. Our data show that the type 2 variant, which allows couples a second child after a girl, results in the highest sex ratios for second order births and the overall highest sex ratios, as seen in Henan, Anhui, Jiangxi, Hunan, Guangdong, and Hainan. These are largely more traditional, predominantly agricultural provinces, where bearing sons is still seen as necessary for long-term security.[21,29]

Although some imaginative and extreme solutions have been suggested, nothing can be done now to prevent this imminent generation of excess men.

Medium sex ratios were most common in the strict type 1 provinces. However, these provinces are also wealthier, levels of education are higher, especially among women, traditional values of preference for sons are changing, and more people have pensions making them less dependent on sons to provide security in old age.[30] A study in 2001 showed that more than 50% of women of reproductive age in such provinces express no preference for a son.[31] The lowest (most normal) ratios are seen in the type 3, most permissive, provinces, such as Tibet, Xinjiang, and Ningxia. However, these provinces are also sparsely populated and poor, inhabited partly by ethnic groups who are generally less inclined to prefer sons and less accepting of abortion.[29]

This analysis is inevitably simplistic, given intra-provincial diversity, but the findings do point to the tendency for the type 2 variant of the policy to result in high sex ratios. The policy implications are clear: Changing the regulations in force in type 2 provinces, which permit most couples a second child after a female birth, could help to reduce the sex ratio. Indeed, some commentators have gone further: Now that the fertility rate is below replacement, some have recommended that all couples should be allowed two children irrespective of sex,[30,31,32] and relaxation of the policy is expected over the next decade.

Although some imaginative and extreme solutions have been suggested[33,34] nothing can be done now to prevent this imminent generation of excess men. The government is very aware of the problem and has openly expressed concerns about the consequences of large numbers of excess men for societal stability and security.[22] As early as 2000 the government launched a range of policies to specifically counter the sex imbalance, the "care for girls" campaign. This includes changes in laws in areas such as inheritance by females, as well as an educational campaign to promote gender equality. These measures have had some success, with reports of lower sex ratios at birth in targeted localities.[22] This shows that change is occurring. In addition, the finding that the sex ratio at birth did not increase between 2000 and 2005, and that the ratio for the first (and usually only) birth in many urban areas is within normal limits, means that the sex ratio may fall in the foreseeable future.

Cite this as: *BMJ* 2009;338:b1211

Contributors: All the authors participated in the analysis and in preparing the tables and saw and approved the final version of the paper. ZWX is the guarantor.

What is already known on this topic

The reported sex ratio (males per 100 females) in China is high, but accurate population-based figures for actual sex ratios have been notoriously difficult to obtain.

The role of sex selective abortion and the influence of the one child policy on the sex imbalance have been unclear.

What this study adds

China will see very high and steadily worsening sex ratios in the reproductive age group for the next two decades.

Sex selective abortion accounts for almost all the excess males.

One particular variant of the one child policy leads to the highest sex ratios.

Funding: This study was funded through a China-UK excellence fellowship for TH from the Department of Innovation, Universities and Skills.

Competing interests: None declared.

Ethical approval: Not needed.

Notes

1. College of Law, Political Science and Public Administration, Zhejiang Normal University, Jinhua, Zhejiang 310347, China.

2. Institute of Social and Family Medicine, Zhejiang University, Hangzhou 310016, China.

3. Centre for International Health and Development, University College London, London WC1N 1EH. Correspondence to: T Hesketh t.hesketh@ich.ucl.ac.uk.

References

1. James WH. The human sex ratio. Part 1: a review of the literature. *Human Biology* 1987;59:721-5.

2. Teitelbaum M. Factors affecting the sex ratio in large populations. J Bio Sci 1970:2:61-71.

3. Arnold F. The effect of son preference on fertility and family planning: empirical evidence. *Popul Bull UN* 1987;23:44-55.

4. Klasen S, Wink C. A turning point in gender bias in mortality? An update on the number of missing women. *Popul Dev Rev* 2002;28:285-312.

5. Sen A. Missing women revisited. *BMJ* 2003;327:1297-8.

6. Hesketh T, Zhu WX. Abnormal sex ratios in human populations: causes and consequences. *Proc Natl Acad Sci USA* 2006;103:13271-5.

7. Park CB, Cho NH. Consequences of son preference in a low fertility society: imbalance of the sex ratio at birth in Korea. *Popul Dev Rev* 1995;21:59-84.

8. Gu B, Roy K. Sex ratio at birth in China, with reference to other areas in East Asia: what we know. *Asia Pac Popul J* 1995;10:17-42.

9. Short SE, Zhai FY. Looking locally at China's one-child policy. Stud Fam Plan 1998;29,4:373-87.

10. Merli MG, Raftery AE. Are births underreported in rural china? Manipulation of statistical records in response to China's population policies. *Demography* 2000;37:109-26.

11. Banister J. Shortage of girls in China today. *J Popul Res* 2004;21:19-45.

12. Johansson S, Nygren O. The missing girls of China: a new demographic account. *Popul Dev Rev* 1991;17:35-51.

13. Zeng Y, Tu P, Gu B, Xu L, Li B, Li Y. Causes and implications of the recent increase in the reported sex ratio at birth in China. *Popul Dev Rev* 1993;19:283-302.

14. Coale A. Excess female mortality and the balance of the sexes in the population: an estimate of the number of missing females. *Popul Dev Rev* 1991;17:518.

15. Attane I. China's family planning policy: an overview of its past and future. *Stud Fam Plan* 2002;33:103-13.

16. Zhang W, Li X, Cui H. China's intercensus survey in 2005. Beijing: China Population Publishing House, 2007.

17. Ulizzi L, Astolfi P, Zonta LA. Sex ratio at reproductive age: changes over the last century in the Italian population. *Hum Biol* 2001;73:121-8.

18. China-Profile. Facts, figures, and analyses. www.china-profile.com.

19. Wu Z, Viisainen K, Hemminki E. Determinants of high sex ratio among newborns: a cohort study from rural Anhui Province. *Reprod Health Matters* 2006;14:172-80.

20. Lofstedt P, Luo SS, Johansson A. Abortion patterns and reported sex ratio in rural Yunnan, China. *Reprod Health Matters* 2004;12:86-95.

21. Chu JH. Prenatal sex determination and sex-selective abortion in rural central China. *Popul Dev Rev* 2001;27:259-81.

22. Li S. Imbalanced sex ratio at birth and comprehensive intervention in China. Presentation at 4th Asia Pacific Conference on Reproductive and Sexual Health and Rights, Hyderabad, 29-31 October 2007. Available at www.unfpa.org/gender/docs/studies/china.pdf.

23. China Population Information and Research Centre. Basic population data of China: 1949-2000. www.cpirc .org.cn.

24. Hesketh T, Zhu WX. The one child family policy: the good, the bad and the ugly. *BMJ* 1997;314:1685-7.

25. Wu ZC, Viisainen K, Wang Y, Hemminki E. Perinatal mortality in rural China: retrospective cohort study. *BMJ* 2003;327:1319-22.

26. Hemminki E, Wu ZC, Cao GY. Illegal births and legal abortions—the case of China. *Reprod Health Matters* 2005;2:5.

27. Li S, Zhu C, Feldman M. Gender differences in child survival in contemporary rural China: a county study. *J Biosoc Sci* 2004;36:83-109.

28. Jha P, Kumar R, Vasa P, Dhingra N. Thirichelvam D, Moineddan R. Low male to female sex ratio of children born in India: national survey of 1.1 million households. *Lancet* 2006:367:211-8.

29. Li R. An analysis of the sex ratio at birth in impoverished areas in China. *Chin J Popul Sci* 1998;10:65-73.

30. Winkler EA. Chinese reproductive policy at the turn of the millennium: dynamic stability. *Popul Dev Rev* 2002;28:379-418.

31. Qu JD, Hesketh T. Family size, sex ratio and fertility preferences in the era of the one child family policy: results from the national family planning and reproductive health survey. *BMJ* 2006;333:371-3.

32. Zeng Y. Options for fertility policy transition in China. *Popul Dev Rev* 2007;33:215-46.

33. Tuljapurkar S, Li N, Feldman MW. High sex ratios in China's future. *Science* 1995;267:874-6.

34. Hudson V, Den Boer AM. A surplus of men, a deficit of peace: security and sex ratios in Asia's largest states. *Int Secur* 2002;4:5-38.

In India, Women Feel Great Pressure to Abort Female Fetuses

Leela Visaria

Leela Visaria is a professor and director of the Gujarat Institute of Development Research in Ahmedabad, India. In the following viewpoint, she argues that Indian women and their families strongly desire sons, because sons care for their parents in old age while daughters go into their husbands' families. At the same time, Indian couples desire smaller families. Thus, readily available ultrasound technology is used to determine the gender of fetuses, and fetuses that are not male are aborted. Visaria argues that laws have done little to prevent this practice and that it can only be changed by altering attitudes toward women in India.

As you read, consider the following questions:

1. What evidence does Visaria provide that the PNDT Act of 1994 did not actually reduce sex-selective abortion?

2. According to Visaria, did mothers-in-law have more of a role in the abortion decisions of high-caste women or low-caste women?

3. How has the female deficit started to affect certain social groups in Gujarat and Haryana, according to Visaria?

Leela Visaria, "Deficit of Girls in India: Can It Be Attributed to Female Selective Abortion?" *Sex-Selective Abortion in India: Gender, Society and New Reproductive Technologies*, edited by Tulsi Patel, Thousand Oaks, CA: Sage Publications, 2007, pp. 69–77. Copyright © Tulsi Patel, 2007. Reproduced by permission of SAGE Publications.

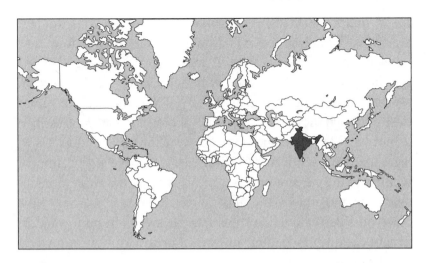

The neglect of and discriminatory behaviour against girls leading to excess female mortality has been widely documented by several studies. But the recent increase in the juvenile sex ratios . . . has very likely resulted from the rapid spread of ultrasound and amniocentesis tests [tests involving the withdrawal of a small amount of amniotic fluid from the womb] for sex determination in many parts of the country, followed by sex-selective abortions. Because of simplicity of the tests and their easy availability on the one hand and strong son preference on the other hand, female-specific abortions appear to have become popular and widely used.

India and Abortion

It is important to understand the emergence of this phenomenon in a wider perspective. India pioneered in legalising induced abortion under the Medical Termination of Pregnancy (MTP) Act, 1971, that specifies the reasons for which an abortion can legally be performed. The act also clearly specifies who can legally perform the abortions and the kind of facilities in which they can be carried out. The stipulated conditions are such that abortions performed by trained doctors who are not registered in facilities not specifically approved for abortion services are termed illegal. According to [researchers] Chhabra and Nuna, in India illegal abortions may be eight to 11 times as high as legal abortions. While the intention is to provide women with safe, legal, timely abortion services, given the stringent nature of the Medical Termination of Pregnancy Act, many safe abortions may be classified as not legal. At the same time, the availability of and access to legal abortion services is so limited for a large proportion of women living in remote rural areas, that in the three decades since the passing of the act, many abortions not only take place outside the ambit of the act, but are often performed in unsafe conditions leading to post-abortion complication and also to death.

Abortion can be legally availed if a pregnancy carries the risk of grave physical injury to a woman, or endangers her mental health or when pregnancy results from a contraceptive failure or from rape or is likely to result in the birth of a child with physical or mental abnormalities. Methods to detect deformities in the foetus [fetus], such as amniocentesis and sonography that use ultrasound technology providing valuable and early information on a range of physical problems, have become available in the country, thanks largely [to] private medical practitioners who are eager to use newer technologies for diagnosis. However, the technologies that help detect physical or mental abnormalities in the unborn child can also identify the sex of the foetus at no extra cost or effort.

India pioneered in legalising induced abortion under the Medical Termination of Pregnancy (MTP) Act, 1971.

Sex Selection and Abortion

There was increasing indirect evidence from some parts of India that termination of pregnancies was resorted not for the reasons stated under the MTP Act, but because there is a strong son preference leading to female-selective abortions.

The gender bias was flagrantly aided by a combination of medical technology that helped detect the sex of the foetus on the one hand and the liberal abortion law that helped couples to abort female foetus on the other. In view of this, the Indian government, responding to the petition made by nongovernmental organisations and women's groups, passed an act prohibiting the practice of prenatal diagnosis of the sex of the foetus (Pre-Natal Diagnostic Techniques [PNDT] Act of 1994). Under the act, individual practitioners, clinics or centres cannot conduct tests to determine the sex of the foetus or inform the couples about it. However, in spite of putting monitoring systems in place, both at the state and the central levels, and with the act in place for six–eight years at the time of the 2001 Census, it is fairly evident that in many places the act has been violated with impunity. Since the two activities of sex detection of the foetus and abortion need not be linked at the stage of using the services, it has become possible to evade the law in connivance with the clinics having ultrasound facilities and doing sonography.

Judging by the hoardings even in small towns and the regular advertisements in the local newspapers and magazines, before the passing of the PNDT Act in 1994, it was evident that clinics conducting sex-determination tests had mushroomed in many towns in the states in the northwestern belt. The open advertisements have now disappeared, but the lucrative practice seems to flourish unabated by simply going underground as evident from the continued decline in the sex ratio of children zero–six years of age. Anecdotal evidence suggests that a strong competition has reportedly led to a reduction in charges for availing these services, which has worked to the advantage of the potential clients. Easy access is, to a certain extent, a response to an increasing demand and female foeticide apparently has replaced the old tradition of culture of neglect of girl child, practice of infanticide among certain communities and sex differentials in the provision of medical care.

Although the release of the 2001 Census results has sparked serious concern about the widespread use of ultra-sound and amniocentesis tests to detect the sex of the foetus, followed by sex-selective abortions, our understanding of many issues around this practice, at the level of the household or from the perspective of women who undergo such abortions, is extremely limited. It is also limited about what actually compels couples or their families to resort to such a practice, who the real decision makers in the family are, [and] what impact does aborting female foetus have on the physical or mental health of the woman who typically undergoes abortion in the second trimester of her pregnancy. Our understanding of how the interlinkages of sex-selective abortion and decline in fertility or in the desired number of children are perceived and articulated is also very limited. The question often raised is: Does the desire for fewer children compel parents to produce children of the sex that they want or that conform to the societal norms and regulate their fertility behaviour accordingly? The qualitative data collected by conducting 44 focus group discussions in which more than 400 women belonging to diverse socioeconomic and educational groups in rural Gujarat and Haryana have provided insights on some of these issues.

Under the act, individual practitioners, clinics or centres cannot conduct tests to determine the sex of the foetus or inform the couples about it.

Son Preference

During the discussions with women both in Gujarat and in Haryana, it was clearly indicated that the majority of the women accepted the outcome of the first pregnancy—whether it was a boy or a girl. However, if the first-born child was a daughter, then the upper caste [that is, upper class, though caste in India is often more rigid and defined than is usually the case with class] women were overtly or covertly pressurised to ensure that the second and or the third child was a boy and to take appropriate measures. Although the women from lower castes experienced this pressure from the family to a much lesser extent, many among them have started either emulating the women from the upper castes or have started thinking the same way.

Thus, the son preference was very evident among all social groups in both Gujarat and Haryana states even when the desired number of children had come down to two or three. No group of women indicated that they would want more than two or three children. They came up with fairly rational explanations about why many children are not desired in the present times and situation. However, in spite of wanting fewer children compared to their parents, women candidly admitted preference for male children. In order to minimise the influence of the other members of the family on the decision of women, women were asked to imagine a hypothetical situation of having all the freedom to choose the number and the sex composition of their children. Among those who indicated that they would like to have three children, the overwhelming response was for two sons and one daughter. However, some who indicated that they would like to have only two children preferred at least one of them to be a son. However, if the two children turned out to be girls then they would almost certainly opt for a third child with a hope that it would be a boy. Women did discuss the possibility that not all sons may support parents in their old age, and yet, the desire for a son was very strong among women of all social groups. As one backward community woman in Gujarat put it:

> Yes, we wait for the son. We must have a son, howsoever he may turn out to be. We would always hope for a son. After all, the daughter will go away after her marriage. The son will stay with us and take care of us.

Women from the upper castes that practise dowry [payment of a sum to the groom's family when one's daughter is married] . . . even voiced that if the first child born to them was a boy, then they would be satisfied with just one child. The menace not of the dowry system but of lifelong presents that have to be given to the girls from the day she marries to her death and also to her children, was a strong deterrent to having girls. Along with that, a fear was articulated that the daughter might be sent back to the parental house if her in-laws were not satisfied with the presents that have been demanded or that she has been given on various occasions by her natal family or for any other reason.

> There is trouble for daughters. They may find a good family or a bad family after their marriage. They [daughters] may come back home. If they have trouble with their in-laws, they may be sent back by their in-laws. In earlier times, the women used to do backbreaking labour, look after the cattle after their marriage. These days, girls do not do that. If there is an economic problem, the in-laws will send the girl back to her parental home. So, a girl is always the reason for the tension of her parents. (Patel [a social group] woman from Gujarat)

> A girl requires a dowry when she has to be married which is a cause for anxiety. Finding a suitable groom and hoping that she will settle down happily in her new home is always a source of worry for parents. (A woman from Haryana)

Yes, we wait for the son. We must have a son, howsoever he may turn out to be. . . . After all, the daughter will go away after her marriage. The son will stay with us and take care of us.

Sex Determination

This almost universal desire for more sons than daughters does get translated in actual behaviour as was evident from the sex ratio of live births. . . . In the focus group discussions also, women from all communities categorically indicated that if the first-born child was a daughter, then the couples would want to and do find out the sex of the next child. Women knew where to go for sex-determination tests, how much the tests cost, etc. They were aware that such tests were not done in public hospitals. One had to go to private facilities, the majority of which according to them also provided abortion services. In fact, almost all women were able to describe the sex-determination procedure quite accurately and in great detail.

Women also indicated that after the birth of a daughter, when they became pregnant again, there was some pressure from the elders in the family to ensure that the next child was a boy. Women themselves also wanted to produce a son. There is a deep internalisation of patriarchal values that are linked to their sense of security. The son preference was internalised to such an extent that women had no hesitation in saying that they would want the sex of the foetus to be known if they had already given birth to one daughter. Although almost all of them had to consult and get permission of their husbands (partly because the sex-determination test involved a cost of a few hundred rupees [around 10–15 dollars]), they themselves saw nothing wrong in finding out the sex of the foetus. As articulated by a Kshatriya [a social group] woman from Gujarat or a Chaudhary woman from Haryana:

> We have to go for the test if the first child is a girl. If we don't go for the test, we may end up giving birth to three or more daughters in the false hope of getting a son.

> Women definitely get the test done . . . if it is a girl they abort the foetus and if it is a boy, they keep the baby. Everybody knows about the test . . . the women themselves want to know whether they are carrying a male or a female child.

Although the parents or parents-in-law of the women very probably had given birth to several children, it appears that they do not wish their daughters-in-law to do so. As the women indicated, the facilities (for sex determination and abortion) did not exist in the earlier times and so the parents had no choice but to bear several children. But in present times, the mother-in-law herself often suggests that the daughter-in-law should get the sex-determination test done, especially after producing one daughter. The parents of the woman, however, generally have no say in the matter, except for wishing that their daughters produce at least one son because their well-being and status in the families of the in-laws depends, to a great extent, on bearing sons.

> *Women from all communities categorically indicated that if the first-born child was a daughter, then the couples would want to and do find out the sex of the next child.*

Mothers-in-law also have changed with the time. They are also aware of the price rise. They might have had raised their several children, but it's difficult to raise more children today. (Backward caste woman from Haryana)

If we already have one son and one daughter, the in-laws would ask us to go in for a test and if it were a daughter, they would even ask us to go in for abortion. (Chaudhary Patel [a social group] woman from Gujarat)

Decision-Making Process About Abortion

When women were asked about the decision-making process if the foetus was found to be that of a female child, the overwhelming response was that after one or two daughters, if the woman was found to be pregnant with another girl, the pressure on her to abort was enormous from her extended conjugal family. Women indicated that the decision to abort a female foetus was almost entirely that of their husbands and/or mothers-in-law. By themselves, women could not make the decision to go in for abortion. Women who had virtually no decision-making power, apparently accepted whatever was desired by her conjugal family, including husbands. They simply accepted and went along with the decision made for them by others. However, we observed some differences between women belonging to higher social groups and those who belonged to scheduled caste and other backward communities with regard to the influence of the in-laws in these matters. High-caste women had to inform and consult their in-laws, but low-caste women had to obtain the consent of only their husbands for abortion. The influence of the extended joint family was not so strong on the decision of the women from lower caste groups.

> A woman cannot make a decision on abortion on her own. If the husband does not want a daughter then he would ask us to go in for abortion. And if he wants a daughter, then we keep the daughter. If the husband is ready to support us and stand by us, we can be firm and go for abortion or not for abortion. In any case, we need to consult our husbands. (Backward caste woman from Gujarat)

> If the first two children are girls and the third one too is a girl then we need to take the permission of the elders to go in for abortion. We have to follow the advice of the elders. (Patel woman from Gujarat)

Women indicated that the decision to abort a female foetus was almost entirely that of their husbands and/or mothers-in-law.

Women also reported that sometimes they themselves desire to abort a female foetus because they already have had one or two daughters. This feeling was stronger among women belonging to social groups such as Patel and Kshatriya, who valued sons much more than daughters. Although they themselves, without much hesitation, would opt for abortion, they still would have to get the permission of the elders of the family to exercise their wish.

Fewer Women, but No Higher Status

The analysis clearly points to a collusion of culture or social norms and technology that is all pervasive. On the one hand, the son preference is so strongly entrenched in Indian society especially in the northwestern region and on the other hand, the well-being and status of girls is so precarious once they are married, that couples avoid having girls at all costs. Facilities conducting sex-detection tests with ultrasound machines have proliferated and are found even in some of the relatively large villages.

Despite the spread of schooling among girls in recent decades, the patriarchal social structure survives. Women derive value and status only as mothers of sons. Their happiness and social status in the conjugal homes is dependent on producing sons. Women have internalised these roles and values to such an extent that even when they say that daughters take better care of parents or are more emotionally attached to the mothers, these statements have a ring of hollowness because in spite of such feelings, more sons than daughters are desired. In the pursuit of sons, they have become, with some pressure from the families, consumers of the new technology of ultrasound, which allows them to choose and bear sons. The possibility of delinking availing legal abortion services from finding and revealing the sex of the foetus provides an opportunity to abort the child of an unwanted sex.

The shift to small family size, evident in India more recently, has not, however, been accompanied by a shift at the same time in the economic and social pressures to have sons and avoid daughters. As was stated by women in both Gujarat and Haryana, they desire and want few children while ensuring that at least one if not two of those children are sons. This has also led to increased acceptance and use of sex-selection tests to achieve parental preferences to have sons while not exceeding the desired number of children.

Women derive value and status only as mothers of sons.

At the same time, the awareness about a ban on sex-determination tests is fairly widespread among women in our study area. Many women also felt that the ban should be removed and couples should have the choice to decide the sex composition of their children. Women were very well aware that the services are easily available from private providers and are within easy access. Government legislation against the use of ultrasound technology for sex detection has only driven it underground and raised the cost, but it is extensively available and used for sex detection. The cost is still affordable and in any case, as many respondents indicated, the cost of the test and related abortion is much lower than the cost of providing dowry and other lifelong presentations to a daughter after marriage. As one of our researchers pointed out: 'The alarm bells ringing in the corridors of power about the missing girls do not find an echo in the dusty by-lanes of the villages of these districts.'

The patriarchal structure and values are ingrained for centuries and the practice of getting rid of daughters is known to exist in these regions such that certain social groups in both Gujarat and Haryana have started feeling the deficit of brides for their sons. According to some women, a few men are forced to remain bachelors and for some, brides are being brought or bought by paying bride price from scheduled tribes and other groups from far away places including other states. We have no hard evidence on the extent of this practice, but it may become a lesson in social integration. However, in spite of the deficit of women, whose impact is being felt in procuring brides, the social norms do not yet seem to be responding.

As is evident, legislation banning the use of sex-determination tests has thus far not succeeded in deterring couples from seeking these tests or preventing the medical practitioners from performing them. The prevalent social norms and practices do raise a number of questions. Is passing of a national legislation to regulate prenatal diagnostic technologies and their misuse an answer? Thus far, the law has been largely ineffective, but will regulatory mechanisms clamped at all levels or better implementation prevent its misuse? Will impounding ultrasound machines in unregistered clinics and to maintain detailed registers about their use in registered clinics help in reducing their use for sex detection of a foetus? We believe, what is needed is a concerted effort to address the bias against girls at the source and changing the underlying conditions that promote sex-selective abortions. However, it is an uphill task and every action and every group that can address this would contribute to improving the status of women in our society.

In the United States, Technology Will Legitimize Sex-Selective Abortion

William Saletan

William Saletan is Slate's *national correspondent and author of* Bearing Right: How Conservatives Won the Abortion War. *In the following viewpoint, he argues that the ease of home fetal gender identification tests is changing attitudes toward sex-selective abortion. At one point, the use of abortion to select sex was seen as immoral, Saletan says, but now the focus has shifted to making sure that the tests sold to determine the sex of a baby are accurate. Saletan argues that the taboo against sex-selective abortion in the United States is eroding, and that soon the practice will be viewed as acceptable.*

As you read, consider the following questions:

1. According to Saletan, how much are prenatal sex tests sold for, and how early can the gender of a fetus be determined?

2. How many prenatal sex tests have led to abortions, as suggested by Saletan?

3. According to the author, what are the Jains willing to do that indicates that they are not ashamed to be seen as using abortion for sex selection?

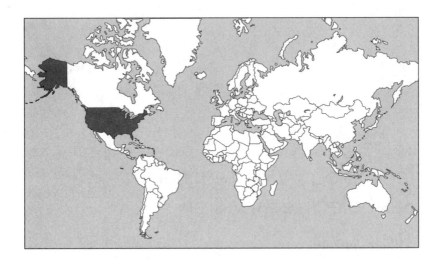

How does a taboo begin to die?

For an answer, look at Sunday's *Los Angeles Times* [February 24, 2008]. . . . The writer, Karen Kaplan, reports that many women are up in arms over home genetic tests that erred in predicting the sex of their kids. More than 100 women are suing one company. Others are calling for regulation.

Normalizing Sex Testing

Why are these women sex testing their fetuses? Kaplan begins with a Canadian couple, Rohit and Geeta Jain:

> She wanted to keep the baby, but Rohit wasn't sure. With two daughters already, the family's finances were a bit strained. Could they really afford a third child?
>
> Geeta countered with another question: What if the baby were a boy?
>
> In traditional Indian culture, sons are prized because they will grow up to manage the family resources and support their parents in old age, even lighting their funeral pyres.
>
> All Geeta had to do was prick a finger and mail a sample of dried blood to the company's laboratory.

Gender Tests in New Zealand

A new test to reveal the gender of a fetus . . . has sparked a row over whether it will lead to sex-selection abortions [in New Zealand].

The . . . IntelliGender test kit, which can be used from eight weeks after conception, [is] to launch in New Zealand within a fortnight [two weeks].

Briony Sowden and Martin Johnston,
"Gender Test Spurs Abortion Fears," New Zealand Herald,
June 8, 2009. www.nzherald.co.nz.

Notice how the new transforms the old. What's old is sex selection: choosing whether to abort your fetus based on whether it's a boy or a girl. What's new is the combination of ease, safety, and privacy with which you can now do this deed.

What's old is sex selection. . . . What's new is the combination of ease, safety, and privacy with which you can now do this deed.

"In the past," Kaplan notes, "virtually all testing was done in medical laboratories for diagnostic purposes, such as searching for the mutations in the BRCA1 gene that are related to breast cancer." Today, however, prenatal sex tests have come down in price to $300 or less, cheap enough to sell directly to would-be parents. And instead of waiting the "10 to 16 weeks needed for traditional medical tests, such as ultrasound," you can now find out at just five to seven weeks whether you're carrying a boy or a girl. That's early enough to get the most basic surgical abortion or, possibly, a chemical abortion instead.

Testing Leads to Abortion

Kaplan's reporting shows how the abortion option looms behind these tests. The Jains considered abortion but decided against it. Another woman "wanted a girl so badly that she and her husband spent $25,000 on in vitro fertilization so that doctors could select female embryos to implant in her womb." The woman took a test at 10 weeks to make sure she wasn't carrying a male fetus. A third woman who got a bogus result from her test says "there are women out there who experience really big disappointment. They really want to give their husbands the little boy they want, or a little girl, and they will abort based on these results."

One company tells Kaplan it has sold 3,500 prenatal test kits. How many thousands more have been sold by other companies? How many of those tests have led to abortions? Nobody knows. And that's the point: Because the test is taken at home, nobody but the couple has to know that the subsequent abortion is for sex selection.

The abortion option looms behind these tests.

But abortion isn't the focus of the article. The focus of the article is that these tests often err. The very idea of elective prenatal sex testing used to be controversial, especially in light of rampant sex-selective abortion in Asia. Now these tests are being bought, used, and reported just like any other prenatal test. The couples who use them are described just as sympathetically. The problem isn't that they're screening their offspring for sex. The problem is that in doing so they're being thwarted by flawed technology and exaggerated marketing.

If you blame the *Times* for this loss of dismay, you're missing the larger trend. The article exists because the underlying stigma has already decayed. Scores of women are suing over erroneous sex tests. The Jains are unashamed to tell their story and put their names on it. So are the other women quoted in the article. As technology makes it possible to break the sex-selection taboo privately and inexpensively, the practice spreads, and we get used to it. The question of whether to restrict it becomes, as with other prenatal tests, a mere question of consumer protection.

Eventually, we'll establish rules to ensure the safety and efficacy of fetal sex tests. At that point, we'll declare them adequately regulated. That's how a taboo begins to die.

Sex Selection That Does Not Involve Abortion Is Ethical

David Heyd

David Heyd is a professor of philosophy at Hebrew University of Jerusalem. In the following viewpoint, he argues that technology is making it possible to select for sex in the fetus without resorting to abortion. Heyd says that this technology harms neither mother nor child. In addition, he argues, there is little evidence that sex selection creates demographic imbalances. Finally, he argues that sex selection does not worsen the status of women in a society. Heyd concludes that sex selection is not morally negative, and that it should be seen as a private choice for parents.

As you read, consider the following questions:

1. According to Heyd, what are some kinds of reasons commonly given for preferring one sex over the other?

2. What methods or practices of sex selection can be seen as problematic or even repugnant, in Heyd's view?

3. According to Heyd, what tactics would be effective in changing the preference against girls in India and what tactics would not be effective?

David Heyd, "Male or Female, We Will Create Them: The Ethics of Sex Selection for Non-Medical Reasons," *Ethical Perspectives* vol. 10, no. 3–4, September–December 2003, pp. 204–214. Copyright © 2003 *Ethical Perspectives*. Reproduced by permission of the publisher and the author.

A dvances in modern medicine have given human beings safer and more reliable methods of birth control, which is the exercise of choice over the number of children we have. But now, with the development of ultrasound technology, amniocentesis, and most recently preimplantation genetic diagnosis (PGD), [all tests for determining the gender of a fetus] we have gained also the ability to choose the sex of the child. We are getting closer to the power to choose at least some elements in the genetic character of future children, and hence their identity, even beyond their gender. To most people, some control over the number of children and the timing of their conception looks morally innocuous, while designing the genetic identity of future children seems morally abhorrent. In between lies the question of sex selection: May we act on the basis of what has become easily accessible information about the sex of a future child?

Sex Selection Is Not Immoral

I would like to argue that from a philosophical perspective, sex selection is a 'non-issue'. Unlike abortion, sex selection does not involve the killing of an allegedly unique human being; unlike human cloning, it does not raise questions as to the nature of reproduction; unlike surrogate motherhood [in which a fertilized egg from a donor is placed in another woman to be carried to term]; sex selection does not force us to revise the notion of parenthood and the institution of the family; and most conspicuously, unlike genetic engineering, it does not give rise to a revision in our deep conception of human identity and the long-term nature of the human genome. This does not mean that there are no moral considerations that should be taken into account when we form an opinion about practices of sex selection; and indeed these considerations will constitute the substance of this [viewpoint]. My only argument is that the extensive treatment of the subject in the last few years, in both public and professional circles, has often had a tendency to over-dramatize, as if sex selection involved radical challenges to traditional conceptions of humanity and reproduction. . . .

The emotionally charged debate about sex selection should be understood against the background of the general reluctance in society to 'play God', to intervene in natural processes, to assume control over what traditionally has been left to fate or luck. Although we often have definite wishes and hopes regarding our offspring, we are not enthusiastic about attaining control over their realization. We regard many aspects of reproduction as processes that 'happen' rather than are chosen and hence tend to a traditional policy of non-interference. The law is typically a conservative system of norms, which is often slow to adapt to new options in reproductive technologies. Thus, most European countries today as well as many other countries in the world prohibit by law the practice of sex selection for non-medical reasons, and are cautious and restrictive about selecting the sex of an embryo on medical grounds.

The most common apprehension about sex selection has to do with the confusion of the choice of sex with the intervention in the human genome [that is, the genetic code]. This is a powerful fallacy that must be dispelled before we engage in the more rational arguments against sex selection. The source of the mistake is easy to detect: Sex is indeed one of the properties that constitute the identity of human individuals, as are other genetic qualities currently studied by genetic science. However, it is obvious that by choosing the sex of a child we do *not* interfere or manipulate the genome in any way, especially when we do so for *non*-medical reasons. Hence, the common concern with a slippery slope leading from sex selection to genetic engineering has no basis in reality and the discussion of the two issues should better be completely separated in both professional and public discussion. Sex selection has nothing to do with eugenics [a belief that the human race can be perfected by preventing the birth of inferior individuals or races] and does not lead to it.

Another related confusion that plays a major role in the debate on sex selection is the allusion to Nazi practices. The alleged slippery slope from sex selection or some forms of genetic screening and engineering to Nazi experiments and mass murder is illusory. The inhumane and cruel treatment of human beings practised by the Nazis was propelled by a racist hatred of Jews, Slavs, Gypsies and other non-Aryan people rather than by a eugenic plan for the betterment of the *human* species. Eugenics preceded Nazi ideology, on the one hand, and Nazi ideology developed mostly independently of eugenic theory, on the other. The wish to choose the sex of one's child is a personal or a cultural preference, which is not related to a eugenic or racist ideal of a world consisting of a single sex.

The common concern with a slippery slope leading from sex selection to genetic engineering has no basis in reality.

Methods of Sex Selection

There is nothing new in the human attempt to decide the sex of future children. The reasons for preferring one sex (usually the male) over the other are of many kinds: economic (work force, the cost of dowries); prestige and inheritance; religious; and psychological (family balancing). Numerous methods have been tried in the course of history, most of which proved ineffective and lacking scientific basis. . . .

Diets, timing of sexual relations, or the sexual positions of the partners have all been suggested as methods for determining the sex of the child. None has proven reliable (or, as the joke goes, they have a 50% chance of success). But it should be noted in the context of our discussion that none of the homemade methods has ever given rise to an opposition on ethical grounds.

Modern science has provided us with a variety of scientifically based methods of determining the sex of the future child. These can be ordered according to the stages in the reproductive process. A pre-conceptive method involves sperm sorting, followed by artificial insemination. In a later stage, in vitro fertilization (IVF) might be used to create a number of fertilized ova out of which those of the desired sex are selected for implantation in the uterus. The most effective way of doing so is by preimplantation genetic diagnosis (PGD) whereby a single cell is removed from an eight-cell 'pre-embryo' and tested for a whole gamut of potential genetic disorders. The sex of the embryo can be easily discovered in this procedure. Ultrasound and amniocentesis are tests undertaken in yet a later stage of gestation and in some societies are used as methods of sex selection. Finally, and unfortunately, sex selection is often practised after birth, usually in the form of female infanticide or abandonment. This last method is of course not a new one and is not related to technological advances. One may also want to add to this list an even later phenomenon, even if not a systematic method, that expresses the preference of one sex to the other, namely the better chances of survival of children of the desired sex who are given better care, nutrition and protection.

This hierarchy of methods of sex selection is of ethical significance. The lower one is on the ladder, the less problematic is the practice from a moral point of view. We have mentioned already that 'folk methods' are not considered morally problematic. The interesting question is whether the lack of opposition to them has to do with their inefficiency or rather with the fact that they are natural. Think of an imaginary DIY [do-it-yourself] set, sold in a pharmacy, which could help couples decide the sex of their offspring: Would that be considered ethically wrong? Legally prohibited? It seems that even if private methods of controlling the sex of the future child were to become effective and reliable, society would not want to interfere in the reproductive freedom of the parents any more than it does in the case of family planning (i.e., decisions about the number of children and their spacing).

Morality and Methods

So it seems that the ethical reservations about sex selection have to do with the *artificiality* of the methods used for its realization and the need for external (medical) assistance. Sperm sorting is indeed a highly artificial procedure that interferes with the natural process of reproduction in a significant way. Its ethical advantage lies, however, in avoiding the controversial issue of abortion, since it precedes the existence of an embryo. No person, even in the most minimal sense, maintained for instance by Catholics, is harmed by this method. And of course there is no risk to the mother either. It is true that the method is not very reliable nowadays, but technically it could in the future become quite easy to apply by couples without the need of any medical assistance.

IVF is different in morally relevant ways. The selection method is performed on fertilized eggs or pre-embryos, some of which are implanted in the uterus, others either destroyed or frozen. Being an invasive procedure, IVF also involves risk to the woman. Unlike 'natural' methods and sperm sorting, which harm no one, IVF affects both existing pre-embryos and the mother. Medical reasons usually justify this procedure, but it leaves open the question whether IVF may be performed for *non*-medical reasons. In order to identify the sex of the future child a genetic test must follow the IVF. Now, assuming that IVF is performed as a matter of medical necessity (e.g., to overcome a fertility problem), should PGD be permitted with the sole purpose of selecting the sex of the child? The more conservative view is that sex selection is justified only if its purpose is of a medical nature, typically to prevent sex-linked diseases. In other words, 'social' sex selection should never be permitted. The more permissive view holds that if IVF has been performed for a medical purpose, there is no reason to prohibit the further PGD test, even if it is carried out just for the sake of selecting the sex of the implanted embryos. A middle approach between the two views is that sex selection could be performed only if there are medical indications for the PGD test, that is to say, selecting sex is legitimate only as a 'side benefit' of a procedure that is independently justified.

[Sperm sorting's] ethical advantage lies . . . in avoiding the controversial issue of abortion. . . . No person, even in the most minimal sense, maintained for instance by Catholics, is harmed by this method.

The conservative view is based either on the slight yet existing risk to the embryo connected with PGD, or on the intrinsic wrongness of sex selection for non-medical reasons. The permissive view maintains that there is nothing wrong *per se* in sex selection and that the risks of PGD (unlike IVF) are minimal and hence do not override the wish of the parents to choose the sex of their child (or specifically decide which of the fertilized eggs, which after all belong to them, should be implanted). The middle way wavers between the two views, respecting the wish of the parents, but doing so only when it does not require taking a specific intentional action.

The conservative view does not seem compelling because the risk in PGD itself is only marginal in a way which does not override either medical reasons such as the prevention of sex-linked hereditary disease or non-medical reasons like parental autonomy. Furthermore, sex selection as such is not morally wrong, since . . . it neither undermines the demographic future of society nor constitutes a stigmatization of women. The middle way, namely applying sex selection only in cases in which PGD is performed for other medical (genetic) indications, does not seem consistent. For if PGD in itself does not involve risk to either the mother or the future child, why should it not be done for gender selection? And if gender selection is illegitimate, why allow it when it is a side benefit? Would it not be a discrimination against women who were not treated for a medical problem and hence are deprived of the right to choose?

Abortion, Infanticide, and Sex Selection

The only argument which carries some weight is that doctors should not engage in practices that are not purely medical (such as sex selection for 'social' reasons). In other words, the moral prohibition on social sex selection is related to the ethics of medical practice and the professional role of physicians, which must be limited to medical treatment. The scarce resources in medicine and the precious time of doctors should not be devoted to non-medical purposes. Unlike harmful genes, gender in itself is not a pathology and hence should not be considered a factor in medical treatment. In response, it should be noted that physicians are nowadays directly involved in a whole spectrum of practices and procedures that are not 'medical' in the traditional sense, be it cosmetic surgery or, closer to our concern, contraception and family planning (including abortions for personal reasons). We do not want physicians to become agents of society in implementing demographic or religious values.

Methods or practices of sex selection in later stages of the development of a human being are undoubtedly more problematic or even repugnant. Many believe that abortion, following ultrasound or amniocentesis tests, is morally controversial and usually justified, if at all, only by serious medical or psychological considerations. A preference for one sex rather than another is hardly such a consideration. Infanticide or the neglect of children of a certain sex is a widespread practice in some societies, but of course can never be justified. But if infanticide is so morally abhorrent, should not abortions such as those performed in some clinics in India be considered the lesser evil? And if such abortions are also considered morally wrong, should we not prefer PGD, which is not an abortion, and does not harm the woman?

From the discussion so far we may conclude that if we look at the hierarchy of the stages of human development we can make the following judgments. Sex selection as part of the sexual act itself is morally neutral, and so is the case of sperm sorting. Performing IVF just for the sake of selecting sex is morally problematic and better avoided because of the risk and pain to the woman. But once IVF is performed for justified medical reasons, further PGD procedure for selecting a male or a female embryo is morally permissible. Abortion for choosing the sex of a child is morally problematic due to both the status of the fetus and the harm to the mother. Infanticide of all kinds is obviously wrong. Now, since folk methods and sperm sorting are far from reliable, we are (at least for the time being) left with PGD as the only permissible and effective means of sex selection.

Infanticide or the neglect of children of a certain sex is a widespread practice in some societies, but of course can never be justified.

However, our analysis so far has taken into account only the interests and rights of the mother, the embryo/future child and possibly the professional duties of the doctor. But the most common arguments against sex selection focus on its impact on society. There are two lines of opposition to sex selection: the demographic and the feminist. We will discuss them in turn.

The Technology of Gender Selection

Matthew and Beth Mandolesi told their doctor that they would be happy with a boy or a girl, but wondered if there was a way to increase the odds that it would be a boy. . . .

The Mandolesi family is part of a growing trend . . . that allows couples to choose their baby's gender. . . .

"A few years ago I had a couple of clients asking every month; now it's at least two or three a week asking seriously about it," said Dr. Kevin Winslow.

A. Chris Gajilan,
"Gender Selection a Reality, but Is It Ethical?"
CNN.com, November 17, 2005. www.cnn.com.

Demographic Imbalance

The principal opposition to the practice of sex selection is based on the fear that it might lead to a dangerous breach of the gender balance in future society. According to this approach, even if sex selection is morally permissible from the point of view of both the future child and the interests and rights of the mother, it should be prohibited on social grounds or in view of the harm to unidentified future people who are going to suffer from the scarcity of partners. The most conspicuous empirical evidence for the rationality of such fears comes from the widespread practice of sex selection in some countries, particularly China and India. Without entering into the widely documented literature on the causes of the clear preference of males to females in these societies, we can say that the prohibition on more than one child per family in China has given rise to female abortions and infanticide so as to guarantee a male offspring. In India, culturally based biases and economic considerations relating to the disastrously ex-

pensive costs of dowries have led to the mass appeal [of] ultrasound tests followed by abortions of female fetuses. Abortions and more recently PGD tests have become more
attractive alternatives to female infanticide that seems to have
been practised for a long time in India.

Without detracting from the repugnance of female infanticide or abortions for the sole purpose of sex selection, it
should be noted that they have been practised for a long time
before the introduction of modern technologies. PGD for sex
selection is not only a morally superior means but also has
only an infinitesimal impact on the demographic balance, at
least for the moment. PGD is an expensive test and requires
an invasive procedure (IVF) which yields only low chances of
live birth (20% on average). Very few women would undergo
this expensive and painful process just for having a boy rather
than a girl. Immigration, for instance, has a much deeper influence on the demographic balance than medically assisted
sex selection, and so do changes in child mortality that affect
the two sexes differentially. Again, it seems that our moral res-
ervation about sex selection is closely related to the active intervention in natural processes rather than to the demographic
imbalance as such.

*So it seems that much of the demographic scare associ-
ated with sex selection is more imaginary than real.*

The concern about the impact of sex selection on the demographic balance should be seen in the wider perspective of
large-scale demographic changes in human history. In her
classic study, the Harvard social historian Marcia Guttentag
analyzes patterns of gender distribution in various societies in
human history and their impact on the status of women in
those societies. Although it appears that there were fairly
sharp differences in the ratio of men and women in certain
societies (in both directions), none of them collapsed for that

reason. Imbalances tend to correct themselves and societies adapt to them through institutional changes in social and legal practices. After all, even in a male-oriented society, men need women for the creation of more men!

Furthermore, the problem of preference for males over females is conspicuous only in certain societies, mainly in East Asia. In contrast, studies show that in most Western countries there is no marked bias towards either of the sexes. Parents usually prefer a 'balanced' family, consisting of children of both sexes. Even in Jewish Orthodox society, in which there is a special premium on a first-born male, once a boy is born, the sex ratio in the rest of the children is of no significant concern.

So it seems that much of the demographic scare associated with sex selection is more imaginary than real. . . .

The last comment on the demographic issue concerns the relation between sex selection and population control. Whether it occurs with the purpose of family balancing or with the purpose of having more children of a particular sex (usually boys), the prohibition on sex selection contributes to population growth. Couples do not stop procreating as long as they do not have a child of a certain sex. If we want to curb population growth, particularly in third world countries, we should allow early stage sex selection (either by sperm sorting or, in the future, by cheap and risk-free IVF and PGD procedures) as a means of satisfying parental wishes in a more responsible way.

Feminism and Sex Selection

Since in most cultures, if there is a marked social preference for one sex it is for the male sex, feminists have naturally associated sex selection with patriarchy, sexist biases, and female subjugation. It is undeniable that female infanticide or abortion for non-medical reasons reflects a general discriminatory attitude to women and that the social status of women in societies in which these practices are widespread is low. The feminist argument is that sex selection, even by means other than infanticide or abortion such as PGD or sperm selection, should be prohibited, since it reflects an androcentric [dominated by masculine interests] view and humiliates women. That is to say, even if there is no medical harm to the mother or to the embryo, the very idea of choosing the sex of children is wrong.

The decrease in the number of women might lead exactly to the increase in their social status, at least in some respects.

Marcia Guttentag, whom we mentioned above, studied in much detail the social implications of imbalanced sex ratios in various societies throughout human history. Her principal hypothesis suggests that the smaller the relative number of women to men, the higher is the status and prestige of women in society. In such societies, monogamy is stronger, although women are expected to fulfill their domestic roles. When the relative number of women increases and becomes larger than that of men (as was the rapid process in American society between the 1940s and the 1970s), women lose their traditional prestige, they become more like sex objects, the number of divorces rises, one-parent families become more prevalent, and more women suffer from depression and suicide. However, in those circumstances more women become ambitious and career-minded.

So the first response to the feminist argument against sex selection is that the decrease in the number of women might lead exactly to the increase in their social status, at least in some respects. But independently of this empirical argument, one can add a second response, namely that personal preference for male or female children does not stigmatize either sex and should not be considered a manifestation of a sexist bias. Personal choice should be clearly distinguished from a systematic social norm, policy, or institutional preference. Personal preference *might* express a gender bias, but by no means must do so. The typical wish parents have for a boy after having three girls does not indicate a male chauvinist attitude. Nor does such a preference manifest a prejudice in other circumstances, such as the wish of a single mother to have a girl rather than a boy, or even the wish of a father to have a son who will carry on his name. None of these preferences expresses in a general way the superiority of one gender to the other.

It is indeed true that some cases of gender preference do indicate a prejudicial and discriminatory attitude. But here we get to the third response to the feminist opposition to sex selection, which might be referred to as putting the cart before the horse. Sex selection does not *create* an anti-women bias; it is a *manifestation* of it. In other words, the way to tackle the problem of sex selection in India is to fight against the deep causes underlying it, to change the social structures and norms that make the birth of girls economically burdensome, like the dowry system. Girls in India are not unwanted as such; they are too expensive for many families to raise. And this can be changed by social reform. Criminalizing sex selection does not address the structural causes that give rise to it. Thus, the current egalitarian attitude to the birth of boys and girls in the West is not the outcome of a prohibition on female infanticide or sex selection, but a manifestation of the more advanced status of women in society, economically, politically, and culturally. In a strange way, the success of the feminist general struggle for gender equality renders the issue of sex selection irrelevant.

Sex Selection Is Unethical Even in the Absence of Abortion

Bart Engelen and Antoon Vandevelde

Bart Engelen and Antoon Vandevelde are professors at the Centre for Economics and Ethics at the Catholic University of Leuven in Belgium. In the following viewpoint, they argue that parents do not own their children, and do not have the right to exercise the extreme control over them that sex selection suggests. They also argue that sex selection may cause demographic imbalances and may result in social justice concerns, since the wealthy would have more access to sex-selection services. For all these reasons, the authors conclude that even when done without abortion, sex selection is immoral.

As you read, consider the following questions:

1. According to the authors, what percentage of implantations lead to live births through in vitro fertilization?

2. How might allowing personal preferences in gender selection lead to a "slippery slope" ethical dilemma, in the authors' view?

3. According to the authors, most people experience the lives of their children not as a matter of individual choice, but as what?

Bart Engelen and Antoon Vandevelde, "The Ethics of Sex Selection for Non-Medical Reasons: A Defence of Common Sense," *Ethical Perspectives*, vol. 11, no. 1, March 2004, pp. 84–87. Copyright © 2004 *Ethical Perspectives*. Reproduced by permission of the publisher and the authors.

In [the September–December 2003 issue of *Ethical Perspectives*] David Heyd defends the permissibility of sex selection for non-medical reasons. He tries to show that there is nothing inherently wrong with this practice and that allowing it does not lead to undesirable consequences. There are several difficulties with his analysis, but the main objection is that it ultimately relies on a crude form of utilitarianism [a philosophical position that moral worth is judged by the happiness or pleasure an action gives to the greatest number of people]. Along with some critical comments on his [viewpoint], we provide ethical arguments in support of the intuitive condemnation of sex selection for non-medical reasons.

Not Morally Permissible

Modern medicine enables us not only to know the sex of our future children, but also to manipulate it. Doctors can artificially fertilize ova and test them for genetic disorders. Using this so-called 'preimplantation genetic diagnosis' one can easily detect the sex of the embryos. As the doctor can select which embryo is implanted by in vitro fertilization, one can freely decide whether one wishes a boy or a girl. In his [viewpoint] David Heyd argues that this procedure for sex selection, together with another pre-conceptive method involving sperm sorting, is morally permissible. We think that this is only the case if the choice is made because of medical reasons. If sex selection is the only means to prevent certain hereditary sex-linked diseases, we see no reason to prohibit such a therapy. We want to show, however, that there are serious ethical problems concerning sex selection for non-medical reasons.

First of all we should recall that, based on the current status of science and technology, sex selection is a very expensive therapy. Moreover, the method based on sperm sorting is still highly unreliable. Also, in vitro fertilization is a risky and painful procedure for the mother and it has a relatively low rate of success: Only 20 per cent of the implanted embryos lead to live birth. Physicians who recently claimed to apply these practices seem to be more in search of a publicity stunt than concerned about the well-being of their clients. These costs and risks probably are the reason why few people actually want to engage in sex selection.

A related problem refers to the fact that sophisticated methods of sex selection are accessible to only the richest segments of society. This diminishes the risk of demographic imbalance caused by extensive appeal to sex selection, but it raises a problem of social justice. Shouldn't government or social security institutions be required to subsidize poor people, thus enabling them to satisfy their wishes concerning the sex of their children? This would require large sums of money. Clearly, such a shift of the financial burden for the satisfaction of these 'expensive tastes' is unacceptable as long as other, more urgent needs remain unfulfilled (such as care for the elderly). Heyd acknowledges that sex selection should not be encouraged, but argues that it should not be forbidden either. According to him, sex selection should be given the same status as aesthetic surgery.

Based on the current status of science and technology, sex selection is a very expensive therapy. Moreover, the method based on sperm sorting is still highly unreliable.

Of course, arguments about costs and risks are wholly contingent, since medical techniques could in the near future prove to become cheaper and more reliable. We should therefore look for more principled arguments in the debate whether sex selection for non-medical reasons is morally permissible or not.

Freedom and Harm

Heyd explicitly endorses a liberal standpoint [based on individual freedom] by stating that "the decision regarding the existence, number and identity of children (. . .) is protected in liberal normative systems as a private matter in which the law representing public interest should interfere only in extreme cases". State regulation is considered illegitimate, because it would unnecessarily restrict the freedom of choice of its citizens. Questions concerning sex selection belong to the private realm of the family or the individual.

A first problem with this kind of analysis is that it is entirely based on the value of increasing one's freedom of choice. It fails to see how the creation of new possibilities to choose from can, paradoxically, reduce one's freedom. When women or couples are able to choose a boy or a girl, increased social and cultural pressure to make a specific choice becomes plausible. As we all know, this is a serious problem in some cultures where girls and women are systematically discriminated against. It is true that modern medicine offers more humane methods of sex selection than infanticide, but it is far from evident that it also enhances human freedom. Heyd misguidedly minimizes the impact of social norms and cultural traditions on the preferences and choices of the individual.

This points to a second and more general problem. Heyd seems to think that personal preferences should be the final touchstone in answering moral questions about sex selection. The danger of this view is that of the 'slippery slope': If the preference to choose a child's sex is reason enough for the moral permissibility to do so, why should this not be the case with other preferences? Why should we not allow the basketball fan to go to the fertility centre asking to 'make' him a two meter high son? We claim that values and not preferences ought to be the main arguments in ethical debates like this.

We should not always slavishly follow the voice of the people or the preferences of some individuals. But what values are at stake here?

Modern medicine offers more humane methods of sex selection than infanticide, but it is far from evident that it also enhances human freedom.

Heyd defends the "permissive view (which) maintains that there is nothing wrong *per se* in sex selection". His strategy is typical of a certain brand of utilitarianism: If you want to defend the interdiction of certain practices, then you should be able to show the harm they would cause. If personal preferences are not racist, sexist or discriminatory, so what? The whole argument consists then in denying or minimizing possible harms caused by the newest methods of sex selection. There is no harm to the child, no harm to society, no abortion, and it makes the parents and the whole family happy. What could then be the problem? One can contest this analysis either by showing that Heyd underestimates a certain harm, or by raising other—non-utilitarian—types of objections against sex selection. We try to do both.

First of all, we think the problem of demographic imbalance to be more serious than Heyd allows. There is ample evidence that the practice of sex selection has not really enhanced the social status of women in India or China, but that it has caused serious problems in many regions of these countries. The struggle against sex selection has become a priority in these countries, especially for defenders of women's rights. Now how can one reasonably struggle against the cheap methods of sex selection used by the lower classes if one permits the wealthy classes to use other methods, more expensive, but supposedly cleaner from an ethical point of view?

Catholic Church Objects to Manipulating Embryos

The Vatican this week [March 2008] included the destruction of embryos on a new list of mortal sins—a particularly pertinent addition given that the Catholic Church in England and Wales is battling controversial new legislation in this very area.

As the Human Fertilisation and Embryology Bill approaches Parliament, the campaign is gearing up.

Sunday masses across the country end with a plea for parishioners to write to their MPs [members of Parliament] with a list of reservations about a bill whose remit ranges from allowing same-sex couples to become joint legal parents of IVF [in vitro fertilisation] babies to creating human-animal hybrid embroys for research.

Clare Murphy, "Catholic Pressure on Fertility Bill," BBC News, March 2008. http://news.bbc.co.uk.

Our Children Are Not Ours

Second, Heyd cannot imagine other, non-utilitarian objections to sex selection for non-medical reasons than those appealing to an outdated form of naturalism. We do think another argument is possible. There is something inherently wrong with the wish to choose the sex of one's own children and this has to do with the fact that this wish is not of the same type as so many other preferences we could have. Although we have lots of wishes and fantasies about our children and their future, we still should realize that our children are not really 'ours'. Parents almost immediately come to be confronted with this experience. Newborn babies cry, even at moments when it does not suit us. Our child, which is so close to us, always re-

181

mains a stranger. Although we want it to become a good student, to have the right friends and to build a decent career, we should realize that it is ultimately up to him or her to make the best out of life. There lies a paradox at the basis of raising a child: We know every day is a surprise, yet we want to remain in control. Desires like these are human and, to a certain degree, relatively unproblematic. The problem is that people sometimes want to gain control to a much higher degree. They wish to control the uncontrollable.

The free choice of the sex of our children is symbolic for this exaggerated search for control. People want to eliminate chance by intervening in the natural processes of reproduction. As Heyd summarizes, the opposition to free sex selection "should be understood against the background of the general reluctance in society to 'play God', to intervene in natural processes, to assume control over what traditionally has been left to fate or luck. Although we often have definite wishes and hopes regarding our offspring, we are not enthusiastic about attaining control over their realization. We regard many aspects of reproduction as processes that 'happen' rather than are chosen and hence tend to a traditional policy of non-interference". Heyd does away with this argument by a sleight of hand and claims that sex selection is not like 'playing God' because we do not have to manipulate the genome itself. This is beside the point. Our argument is more fundamental since it appeals to our basic feelings about the role we are to fulfill in this world. Is our life—and that of our children—the result of our individual choices? Or do we experience the lives of ourselves and our children in the first place as a gift? People who sympathize with this latter view usually situate themselves in a transcendent reality, or at least in a universe which is larger than oneself. This is sometimes thought of as some theistic being, but this need not always be the case.

This argument is, in our opinion, the most important one in the debate about sex selection for non-medical reasons, although it is also the most controversial one. We can understand that not everybody finds it convincing. We are referring here to the most fundamental views people have about the world and their place in it. While proponents of free sex selection will continue to argue in favour of it in terms of individual autonomy and utility, we fundamentally reject their underlying individualistic view of society. Furthermore, we posit that this rejection motivates the basic moral intuitions of the majority of the people in modern-day Western societies in their opinion of sex selection.

Free sex selection is a subversion of the meaning of the authentic wish to have children.

Against Technocracy

This does not mean that an ethical debate about sex selection is impossible. We are simply stating that one should allow for all sorts of arguments, instead of trying to decide the debate on purely utilitarian or consequentialist considerations. Mostly these fail to understand the long-term consequences of broad societal and cultural trends. The intrusion of the wish to gain absolute control in the most intimate spheres of our lives is such a trend, one whose consequences can hardly be foreseen. A more serious problem is that non-utilitarian arguments referring to, say, symbolic meanings tend to disappear from the public debate. Our purpose was to revive one of those arguments by showing that free sex selection is a subversion of the meaning of the authentic wish to have children. The intuitive rejection of free sex selection by most people relies on forms of non-utilitarian reasoning that should in our opinion be taken more seriously in ethical debates.

Finally we want to object to the idea that society should always swiftly adapt to scientific and technological progress. The idea that everything that is technically feasible should be implemented, from the moment that there is an economic demand for it, and no matter what objections people intuitively raise against it, is the very essence of technocracy. Maybe Heyd is right in arguing that in ten years' time the methods of sex selection he advocates will have become a widespread practice, but as moral philosophers should know, not all factual developments are desirable. This seems to us an example of an illegitimate inference from 'is' to 'ought'.

Periodical Bibliography

The following articles have been selected to supplement the diverse views presented in this chapter.

Dave Andrusko — "Sex-Selection Abortion and Pro-Abortion Feminists: Caught on the Horns of a Dilemma," National Right to Life, February 27, 2009. www.nrlc.org.

Scott Baldauf — "India's 'Girl Deficit' Deepest Among Educated," *Christian Science Monitor*, January 13, 2006. www.csmonitor.com.

Stephen Clarke — "Sex Selection & Abortion: Canada," Law Library of Congress, June 2009. www.loc.gov.

Steven Ertelt — "China Gender Imbalance Increases as Sex-Selection Abortions Continue," LifeNews.com, September 27, 2006. www.lifenews.com.

Clare Feikert — "Sex Selection & Abortion: Australia," Law Library of Congress, June 2009. www.loc.gov.

Sam Roberts — "U.S. Births Hint at Bias for Boys in Some Asians," *New York Times*, June 14, 2009. www.nytimes.com.

William Saletan — "Fetal Subtraction: Sex Selection in the United States," *Slate*, April 3, 2008. www.slate.com.

William Saletan — "Sex Reversal: Child Quotas, Abortion, and China's Missing Girls," *Slate*, April 15, 2009. www.slate.com.

Briony Sowden and Martin Johnston — "Gender Test Spurs Abortion Fears," *New Zealand Herald*, June 8, 2009. www.nzherald.co.nz.

Lisa Wade — "*New York Times* Frames Sex Selection as Culturally 'Asian,'" *Sociological Images*, June 22, 2009. http://contexts.org.

GLOBALVIEWPOINTS

CHAPTER 4

Abortion and
Sex Education

In South Africa, Women Need to Be Taught That Abortion Is Legal

Chelsea Morroni, Landon Myer, and Kemilembe Tibazarwa

Chelsea Morroni, Landon Myer, and Kemilembe Tibazarwa are professors at the University of Cape Town in South Africa. In the following viewpoint, they note that abortion under many circumstances is legal in South Africa. However, the authors' survey results show that as many as a third of women in South Africa do not realize that abortion is legal. The authors conclude that women in South Africa need to be provided with better information about the availability of legal abortion.

As you read, consider the following questions:

1. Under what circumstances are abortions legal in South Africa, according to the authors?

2. According to the authors, what was the median age and level of education of the women in their study?

3. According to the authors, why does knowledge about abortion vary so much from clinic to clinic, and what should be done about this?

Chelsea Morroni, Landon Myer, and Kemilembe Tibazarwa, "Knowledge of the Abortion Legislation Among South African Women: A Cross-Sectional Study," *Reproductive Health*, vol. 3, August 3, 2006. Copyright © 2006 BioMed Central Ltd. Reproduced by permission.

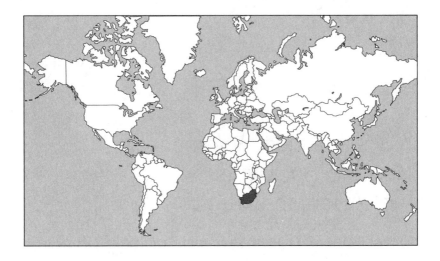

Experiences from around the world show that restrictive abortion laws lead women to have unsafe abortions, in turn contributing to over one-tenth of maternal deaths in developing countries. Before liberalization of the South African law in 1996, about 1,000 legal abortions were granted annually in South Africa, mostly to middle- and upper-class white women. At the same time, roughly 200,000 unsafe abortions were performed annually, the vast majority among poor black women, resulting in an estimated 45,000 hospital admissions and over 400 deaths from septic abortions [abortions involving infection of the uterus] each year. The 1996 Choice on Termination of Pregnancy Act gives women in South Africa the right to choose whether or not to have a safe abortion. As a direct result of this legislation, abortion-related morbidity and mortality have plummeted across the country. However, abortion services still remain inaccessible to many women because of stigma, provider resistance, and lack of trained providers and facilities certified by the national or provincial department of health to provide abortions, especially in rural areas; as a result, illegal abortions still occur.

A Time-Restricted Health Service

Abortion is a time-restricted health service: The act states that a pregnancy may be terminated upon a woman's request during the first 12 weeks of gestation, beyond 12 weeks and up to 20 weeks for reasons of adverse effects on the woman's mental or physical health or socioeconomic status, in cases of rape and incest, and in cases where the fetus would suffer from severe physical or mental abnormality. From 20 weeks onward, terminations are available under very limited circumstances. Because of these time restrictions, for this law to fully achieve its goal of improving reproductive health by allowing a woman to decide whether and when to reproduce, women must know that abortion is a legal and accessible option in the case of unwanted pregnancy, ideally *before* they become pregnant. Moreover, women need to be aware of the time constraints involved, as well as how and where to access abortion services. This study investigated knowledge of the abortion legislation eight years after the introduction of legal abortion services in South Africa among women attending primary care public health clinics in the Western Cape Province, South Africa.

Assessing Women's Knowledge

To assess women's knowledge of key reproductive health services, including abortion, emergency contraception (EC) and voluntary testing and counselling for HIV, in 2004/2005 we undertook a cross-sectional study in 26 community health clinics in one urban and one rural health region in the Western Cape Province, South Africa. The Western Cape is among South Africa's better-resourced provinces, with the largest number of positive reproductive health indicators, and is considered to have the best-developed reproductive health infrastructure in the country. The study was requested by the Western Cape provincial health department. Here we report on women's knowledge about abortion legislation. . . .

Of the 831 women who participated (628 urban participants and 203 rural participants), most were attending the clinic on the day of the interview for medical complaints (37%), antenatal or postnatal care (32%), or family planning services (21%). The median age was 28 years and the median level of education was grade 10. Most participants spoke either Afrikaans or Xhosa as their main language (47% and 44%, respectively). Of the 688 participants who had ever been pregnant, 61% reported that their last pregnancy was unintended.

Overall, 32% of women did not know that the law in South Africa allows for legal abortion, and this proportion was substantially higher in the rural region (40%) compared to the urban region (29%). Furthermore, from clinic to clinic, the proportion who knew abortion was legal ranged from less than 6% to more than 64%. Among the 567 respondents who were aware of legal abortion, almost half (48%) did not know there was a time restriction for a legal termination of pregnancy on request (without restriction). Of the 295 participants who knew that there was a time restriction, 20% thought that it was 12 weeks or less, 4% thought that it was more than 12 weeks, and 76% did not know what the time restriction was. Of those who were aware of legal abortion, only 9% had ever discussed abortion with a health care worker.

One-third of women surveyed do not know that abortion is legal in South Africa.

Of the total sample, most women perceived legal abortion in the first trimester by manual vacuum aspiration [a common abortion method] as medically safe (62%) and believed that women should be allowed to have a legal abortion upon request (63%). A substantial minority of women (38%), however, considered legal abortion to be an unsafe procedure, and most commonly mentioned concerns about a reduction in future fertility as the reason. . . .

One-Third Do Not Know

This is one of the few studies focusing on South African women's knowledge of the abortion law. These findings show that one-third of women surveyed do not know that abortion is legal in South Africa. Knowledge of the legality of abortion in other similar settings where abortion is legal in some form ranges from 45% in Mexico to 57% in Latvia to 78% in the Gauteng Province of South Africa. In one qualitative study of South African women who had abortions outside of the legal abortion services, 54% reported having done so because they did not know about the law. The 1998 South African Demographic and Health Survey (DHS), which was conducted less than two years after the implementation of the Choice on Termination of Pregnancy Act, found that nationally 53% of women knew of legal abortion; the Western Cape provincial figure was 51%. In this study, 68% of women knew that abortion is a legal health service. Although this study used the same questions as the DHS, the DHS figures are not directly comparable to these findings due to different sampling methodologies: The DHS was a community-based sample of women and this study sampled women attending health services. A comparison of these two sets of data suggests that more women know about legal abortion now than did in 1998. However, another explanation for this apparent difference in levels of knowledge is that this survey was conducted among individuals attending public health clinics, with greater access to health education. Thus, the 2004/2005 results may simply reflect greater knowledge in this sample compared to the general population of the Western Cape, as opposed to an increase in knowledge among all women through time. In general, it is likely that awareness of abortion legislation in

Knowledge of Abortion by Characteristic Among Those Surveyed at a Cape Town Health Clinic

This table shows characteristics and knowledge of the women surveyed by the authors of this viewpoint.

Characteristic, %	Know That Abortion Is Legal	Do Not Know That Abortion Is Legal
Total	68.7	31.3
Region		
Urban region	71.5	28.5
Rural region	60.3	39.7
Age (years)		
15–19	68.3	31.7
20–29	68.7	31.3
30–39	67.0	33.0
40–49	75.2	24.8
Education		
Less than secondary school	62.6	37.4
Secondary school or above	69.4	30.6
Marital status		
Married	67.0	33.0
Unmarried	70.0	30.0
Method used at last sexual intercourse		
No method	65.0	35.0
OC/injectable/sterilization	80.0	20.0
Male condom/female condom	79.5	20.5

Chelsea Morroni, Landon Myer, and Kemilembe Tibazarwa, "Knowledge of the Abortion Legislation Among South African Women: A Cross-Sectional Study," Reproductive Health, *August 3, 2006.*

this clinic-based sample in the Western Cape Province, which has a better reproductive health infrastructure than most other areas of the country, is higher than in the general population of South Africa.

These data suggest that approximately one-third of the women we surveyed in 2004/2005 do not know that abortion is legal in South Africa. This finding, coupled with the findings that 61% of last pregnancies in this sample were unintended and 25% of women who did not want to fall pregnant did not use contraception during last intercourse, is worrisome. Not only are an appreciable proportion of these women uninformed about the option of abortion in the case of unwanted pregnancy, they are also unable to protect themselves from unintended pregnancy in the first place. This study shows that lack of knowledge of legal abortion is associated with lack of other reproductive health knowledge, such as awareness of EC [emergency contraception, which can be taken shortly after intercourse] and contraceptive use. Thus, the 32% of women who do not know that abortion is a legal option may be the women at greatest risk for unwanted pregnancy.

Furthermore, this study reveals tremendous variability from clinic to clinic in terms of women's knowledge of the abortion legislation. Reasons for this inter-clinic variability are poorly understood. This is a key finding that requires further research so that the health services are able to appropriately target certain clinics and areas for intervention.

Given that only 9% of those aware of the law had ever discussed abortion with a health care worker, there is clearly a need for greater client-provider dialogue regarding abortion, particularly the time restrictions and safety of the legal procedure. Regardless of individual provider beliefs, relaying basic information on the legality of abortion may need to become part of routine reproductive health counselling.

In addition, community-based health information campaigns and school-based sex education and life skills programs should incorporate information on abortion services. Expanding access to information about abortion beyond the clinic setting is essential in that women who are at highest risk for unintended pregnancy and therefore for abortion—women who cannot or do not access family planning services—are unlikely to visit a health care provider who could discuss the law with them.

This study shows that lack of knowledge of legal abortion is associated with lack of other reproductive health knowledge.

Overall, these findings indicate that there is a substantial unmet need among women for information on abortion. Strategies should be developed to address this gap so that women are fully informed of their rights to a safe and legal termination of pregnancy. For the abortion legislation to fully contribute to improve health in South Africa, all South African women must know that abortion is a legal and accessible option in the case of unwanted pregnancy.

In Russia, Poor Sex Education Results in Too Many Abortions

Chloe Arnold

Chloe Arnold is the Moscow correspondent for Radio Free Europe/Radio Liberty. In the following viewpoint, she explains that contraception in Russia is expensive and sometimes unreliable, and that sex education is not taught in school. As a result of these factors, Arnold concludes, abortion is a preferred means of birth control in Russia. Arnold reports that this can be physically and psychologically damaging to women. She suggests that more education is needed to teach women about options other than abortion and to educate them about some of the dangers of abortion procedures.

As you read, consider the following questions:

1. According to Arnold, how many abortions and live births were there in Russia in 2006?

2. How many women in Russia use birth control pills as their primary form of contraception, according to Arnold?

3. What demographic factors make the Russian government eager to reduce abortions, according to Arnold?

Chloe Arnold, "Abortion Remains Top Birth-Control Option in Russia," Radio Free Europe/Radio Liberty, June 28, 2008. Copyright © 2008 RFE/RL, Inc. All rights reserved. Reprinted with the permission of Radio Free Europe/Radio Liberty, 1201 Connecticut Ave., N.W. Washington DC 20036. www.rferl.org.

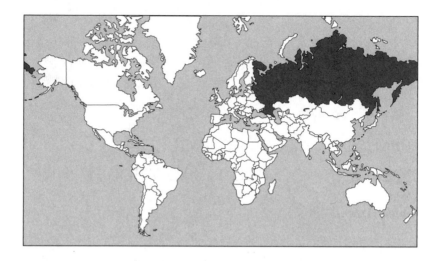

Dilyara Latypova is a gynecologist in the Russian republic of Tatarstan. With more than 25 years of experience, she's seen some progress in family planning since the days of the Soviet Union, when such topics were largely taboo.

Abortion as Family Planning

Still, she says, the situation today is far from ideal. For many women, the most common method of birth control remains a Soviet-era holdover: abortion.

"Young women who think that having an abortion is an easy thing are wrong," Latypova tells RFE/RL's [Radio Free Europe/Radio Liberty's] Tatar-Bashkir Service. "An abortion is not only an operation. It's a deep psychological trauma for a woman. This is an operation that causes a woman physical and moral pain. I don't think it's the right decision."

Despite an abundance of new family planning options, Latypova says lack of public awareness and prohibitive expenses—like $25 monthly packs of birth control pills—mean many women still see abortion as their only choice.

"Students and young girls can't afford birth control. Many girls are afraid to talk about it with their mothers and ask for money," she says. "An unplanned pregnancy can cause them enormous stress. They immediately opt for an abortion, and don't even tell their parents or boyfriends."

Lack of public awareness and prohibitive expenses . . . mean many women still see abortion as their only choice.

Russia was the first country in the world to legalize abortion, in 1920. The procedure was briefly driven underground, when Soviet leader Joseph Stalin banned abortion in an attempt to encourage women to have larger families.

But after Stalin's death in 1953, the ban was lifted. A decade later, the practice had become so common that the USSR [Union of Soviet Socialist Republics] officially registered 5.5 million abortions, compared to just 2 million live births.

Easily Available Abortions

The number of abortions has fallen dramatically since then. The most recent available figures, for 2006, show 1.6 million abortions compared to 1.5 million live births—a dismal figure, especially in a country struggling with a looming demographic crisis [that is, with a population that is falling rapidly].

Women are entitled to abortions up until the 12th week of pregnancy, and—unlike in many countries—are not obligated to alert relatives or give a reason for requesting the procedure.

The relative ease of getting an abortion, in fact, has blinded many women to the numerous health risks associated with the process, especially for those who turn to it more than once. "The complications include bleeding and inflammation in the short term," says Lyubov Yerofeyeva, the director of the Russian Family Planning Association, an NGO [nongovernmental organization] that works to improve sex education in Russia. "In the long term, the most severe complication could be infertility."

Yerofeyeva is speaking in a brightly lit office in central Moscow whose walls are adorned with posters of cuddly babies. But Yerofeyeva and other association employees can also paint a stark picture of the reality of abortion in Russia today.

Sex education is not part of the national curriculum in Russia. So when most young people become sexually active, at around the age of 16, Yerofeyeva says they know almost nothing about how women become pregnant.

When most young people become sexually active . . . they know almost nothing about how women become pregnant.

"You can't say the idea of family planning and birth control is flourishing," she says. "The tradition in Russia is not to talk about sexuality loudly, not to tackle these issues—even within a family, even between husband and wife. Sometimes they're not even communicating about their own sexual relations. These issues have always been very closed."

Growing Options

Part of the reason abortions were so prevalent during the Soviet era, health professionals say, was that contraceptives were so unreliable. Oral contraception was not available and more often than not, Soviet-made condoms and intrauterine devices [IUDs] didn't work.

In the years after the Soviet collapse, before the expense grew too great, some gynecological clinics attempted to provide birth control for free, a practice that has proved successful in places like the United Kingdom. The number of Russian women who use the pill as their primary form of birth control remains low—between 3 and 13 percent as compared to 52 percent in Europe. The predominant form of preventive birth control is the highly uncertain rhythm method [that is, couples attempt to have sex only when the woman is least fer-

Russia's Demographic Decline

The Russian population has been falling since the early 1990s.

A UN [United Nations] report recently [October 2009] published its verdict on Russia's demographic situation. In 1950, what is now the Russian Federation had the fourth largest population in the world, but by 2007, it ranked 9th globally, behind Bangladesh and Nigeria. By 2050, the UN estimates, the Russian population will have fallen behind that of Vietnam.

The Russian population has fallen by 6.6 million since 1993, despite a large influx of immigrants that has made Russia the second most popular destination for labor migrants in the world after the United States. The UN estimates the country could lose a further 11 million people by 2025. Such vast losses are only comparable to wartime.

Ben Judah,
"Russia: Ominous Demographics,"
ISN, October 14, 2009, www.isn.ethz.ch.

tile]. But Vladimir Shchigolev at the Moscow office of the World Health Organization says the situation is improving.

"At the moment, the younger generation knows more about family planning, and they have better access to family planning services. Today, they can go to the pharmacy and buy contraceptive pills, condoms, modern IUDs that are quite different from Soviet IUDs—they are absolutely safe," Shchigolev says. "Of course they talk about abortion, but they talk about abortion as not a good way to prevent pregnancy and to plan a family."

Abortion techniques have come a long way since the Soviet era, when 35-year-old Olga Lipovskaya related her experience in Francine du Plessix Gray's acclaimed book *Soviet Women: Walking the Tightrope.*

Olga Lipovskaya estimated that she had had about 14 abortions in total, and she knew women who had had as many as 25.

"You stand in line before the door of the operating room, waiting to be taken in," she says. "Then it's your turn, and you go into a hall splattered with blood, where two doctors are aborting seven or eight women at the same time; they're usually very rough and rude. If you're lucky they give you a little sedative."

According to du Plessix Gray, Olga estimated that she had had about 14 abortions in total, and she knew women who had had as many as 25.

Psychological Trauma

Today, modern techniques make the experience less traumatic and dangerous, but Natalia Vartapetova, the director of a Russian NGO called the Institute of Family Health says complications following abortions are still widespread.

"Unfortunately, still, the consequences of abortion are among the key causes of maternal mortality in Russia," she says. "One of the problems, perhaps, is infection control—infection and sepsis [whole body inflammation caused by a toxic bacterial infection] afterward—or other complications, like hemorrhage. Infertility, as well—we know about one-third of infertility is due to previous abortions."

But for all that, the situation is improving, Vartapetova says. One of her projects is to educate health professionals about modern methods of birth control, and in the 20 or so regions where the programs are taking place, abortion rates have fallen.

And with the population level in severe decline—demographers estimate it could fall below 100 million by 2050, from 150 million in 1992—the Russian government is also keen to tackle the issue of abortion. Last year [2007], then president Vladimir Putin introduced a long-term project to encourage women to have families with more than one child.

"Unfortunately, still, the consequences of abortion are among the key causes of maternal mortality in Russia," she says.

The pro-Kremlin youth group Nashi this year staged a demonstration to protest abortion, adorning rows of cemetery-style crosses with signs reading "architect," "driver," "editor," and other professions—a nod to the potential labor lost to terminated pregnancies. (Nashi's conservative social streak extends to birth control; the group has protested against condoms and other preventive family planning methods.)

Vartapetova warns that attempts to prevent abortions or to restrict access to birth control would be a mistake. "When we talk about the demographic crisis, quite often there's a misunderstanding—that family planning leads to smaller family size. International evidence that shows that that's not true—and that family planning actually improves women's health and decreases abortion rates. But this information isn't that well known among our policy makers."

Doctors like Latypova in Tatarstan are also quick to remind women of the enormous emotional cost that abortion can inflict. While the topic of abortion does not spark the kind of fierce moral debate seen in countries like the United States, Latypova says terminating a pregnancy can be a devastating experience.

"You can't compare the emotional state of a woman who undergoes an abortion with anything else. As both a doctor and a mother, I can say that it's a huge psychological trauma.

There are very few women who can just breezily say, 'Oh, I had an abortion.' I think there's no abortion that doesn't leave its mark on a woman."

In Zimbabwe, Poor Education Results in Too Many Illegal Abortions

IRIN

IRIN (Integrated Regional Information Networks) is a news project of the United Nations that focuses on humanitarian news in underreported regions of the world. In the following viewpoint, it reports that Zimbabwe has restrictive abortion laws and many women have little knowledge of contraception. As a result, IRIN argues, illegal abortion is a serious problem that kills many women each year. The country is unlikely to liberalize its abortion laws, IRIN concludes, so better sex education is urgently needed.

As you read, consider the following questions:

1. According to IRIN, what must a woman who is raped in Zimbabwe do in order to obtain an abortion?
2. According to UNICEF, what is the average age at which youth in Zimbabwe begin to be sexually active?
3. Why is legalization of abortion unlikely in Zimbabwe, according to IRIN?

An estimated 70,000 illegal abortions take place in Zimbabwe every year, says a [2005] report by the UN [United

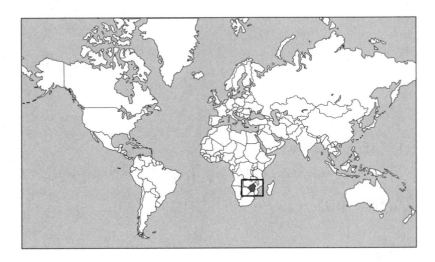

Nations] Children's Fund (UNICEF). The UN agency called for a national education drive to raise awareness of sexual and reproductive health.

Abortion Restrictions

According to UNICEF's *Children and Women's Rights in Zimbabwe—Theory and Practice*, legal abortion is permitted only under certain circumstances, making it very difficult to access. The Termination of Pregnancy Act of 1977 permits the procedure when the life of the woman is endangered, the child may suffer a permanent physical or mental defect, or the foetus [fetus] was conceived as a result of rape or incest. Termination may take place only at a designated hospital, with the written permission of the hospital superintendent; in cases of suspected birth defects, or life and death situations, the authority of two medical practitioners is also required. For rape, a certificate by a magistrate is needed, and is issued only after consideration of a police report and an interview with the victim. The laborious process of satisfying these conditions, coupled with the fact that legal abortions are not free, have led to a growing 'black market' for the procedure, where backstreet terminations are often performed by unskilled personnel in

unhygienic surroundings. Illegal, self-inflicted abortion methods are thought to include the consumption of detergents,
strong tea, alcohol mixes and malaria tablets; other methods
include the use of knitting needles, sharpened reeds and hang-
ers.

The health ministry began a post-abortion care programme five years ago at the Harare and Parirenyatwa hospitals, two of the country's largest referral centres, to care for
women suffering from induced and spontaneous miscarriage.
Tsungai Chipato, one of the programme doctors, said on average between six and 10 women were treated daily at each institution. Professor Jonathan Kasule, from the Obstetrics and
Gyaenocology Department of the University of Zimbabwe's
Medical School, told IRIN [a UN news agency] that the bulk
of patients seeking help at the post-abortion care centres were
in the 15 to 24 age group. "They come in bleeding, with septic
reeds stuck in their private parts, and if you do not immediately work on them, they die—it is one of the commonest
causes of maternal mortality," he said.

Education Needed

Edna Masiiwa, director of Women's Action Group (WAG),
told IRIN that knowledge of the abortion law was vague and
few women were aware of the post-care abortion programme.
Kasule pointed out that people were also generally unaware of
the emergency or morning-after pill, Postinor-2 [which can
terminate pregnancy shortly after conception], available at
pharmacies. UNICEF noted that the onset of sexual activity
among the youth in Zimbabwe occurred at an average age of
14, but they were often uninformed where pregnancy was
concerned. The report said a 1999 survey indicated that "25
percent of youth think that a girl could not get pregnant the
first time she has sex, and 40 percent believe that a girl cannot
get pregnant if she has sex standing up". Masiiwa added that
for girls the first sexual encounter was normally "unplanned".

According to the report, adolescents participating in the survey said most of them used abortion as a family planning method, "due to the difficulties encountered in accessing family planning services". Service providers tended to rely on national laws and policies that generally upheld parental consent requirements for adolescents; adults commonly believed that access to contraception and information about it promoted promiscuity; married adolescents could access contraceptives more easily than their unmarried counterparts, all of which contributed to the stigma involved in accessing contraception. Kasule said Zimbabwe's uptake of oral contraception was relatively high—56 percent—but there was still a significant gap.

"25 percent of youth think that a girl could not get pregnant the first time she has sex, and 40 percent believe that a girl cannot get pregnant if she has sex standing up."

Masiiwa said sex education in schools needed to be stepped up to make girls aware of the conventional contraceptive options available. Her organisation had run a programme in Beitbridge, on the South African border, where, "in 2005 few were even aware of the female condom and yet it was introduced in the late 1990s". She stressed that use of the male condom also had to be promoted. Broader abortion legalisation was thought to be unlikely, as the country was largely Christian and conservative, with a strong pro-life lobby. [Law professor Geoff] Feltoe believes that even if abortion were to be legalised, Zimbabwe lacks the medical facilities to handle large-scale lawful termination. "Abortion would be a low priority in the context of things," he told IRIN. "There is already huge stress on the current health facilities, and it would meet resistance from nurses and other health staff."

In Scotland, High Abortion Rate Suggests Failure of Sex Education

Magnus Gardham

Magnus Gardham is the political editor of the Daily Record. *In the following viewpoint, he reports that Scotland has a high abortion rate, with even relatively young adolescents receiving abortions. Gardham argues that the government's efforts to combat teen pregnancy through changes in sex education seem to be failing and should be reevaluated.*

As you read, consider the following questions:

1. According to Gardham, how many girls under sixteen had abortions between 2001 and 2009 in Scotland?
2. According to Susan Deacon, it might be preferable to have thirteen-year-old girls have what if it would prevent them from becoming pregnant?
3. According to Gardham, what are students in Scottish schools taught in their sex education classes?

Abortions are being carried out on dozens of girls aged just 12 and 13 in Scotland.

Figures obtained by the [*Daily*] *Record* under Freedom of Information show eight 12-year-olds and 87 13-year-olds have had abortions in the last nine years.

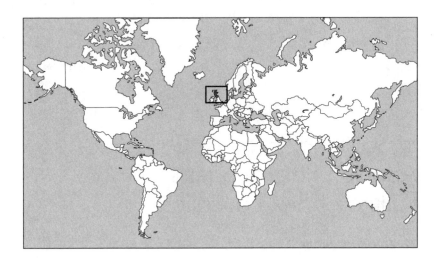

Hundreds of girls aged 14 and 15 have also had abortions during the same period.

Too Many Abortions

The Catholic Church in Scotland last night [August 2009] described the figures as "appalling and distressing."

The revelations sparked calls for changes to sex education in Scotland's schools.

The sex education strategy, launched by Labour [a Scottish political party] and now backed by the SNP [Scottish National Party], was designed to cut teenage pregnancy rates by a fifth. But there is little chance that target will now be met by next year's deadline.

NHS [National Health Service] Scotland provided the most detailed figures ever seen for abortions carried out on very young girls in response to *Daily Record* questions. Before today, the NHS only gave figures for the number of abortions carried out on all under-16s.

But we can reveal 13 girls under the age of 14 had an abortion last year. A further 82 14-year-olds terminated pregnancies. And 248 girls aged 15 had abortions.

Figures showed eight 12-year-olds and 87 13-year-olds had abortions between 2000 and 2008. In the same period, 695 14-year-olds, 2,081 15-year-olds and 4,509 16-year-olds had abortions.

It adds up to a total of 2,871 abortions performed on girls under 16—the legal age of consent—in the last nine years. Separate NHS figures show 2,528 girls under the age of 16 gave birth between 2000 and 2007.

In recent years, more under-16s have chosen to terminate a pregnancy than have their babies.

Former health minister Susan Deacon, who was the driving force behind Scotland's sexual health strategy, said children needed better advice and support—including access to contraception.

But she stressed government strategies alone could not solve a problem deeply rooted in social problems and a "lack of love and nurture" in the lives of many young girls.

She said: "I have no hesitation in saying we should do more to encourage young people to delay sexual relationships. But a lot of young people are going to have sex. In some cases, it will be appropriate to offer more and better contraceptive solutions for these girls.

In recent years, more under-16s have chosen to terminate a pregnancy than have their babies.

"Yes, they are under the age of consent. But you have to boil it down to this—would you rather these young people get pregnant or not?

"Some people would find it morally reprehensible for a 13-year-old girl to have a contraceptive implant, for example, but in limited circumstances and with appropriate support and supervision isn't that preferable to becoming pregnant?"

Abortion Rates per 1,000 Women, Ages 15–44, in Scotland, by Year

Year	Rate
1999	11.2
2000	11.1
2001	11.3
2002	11.1
2003	11.6
2004	11.8
2005	12.0
2006	12.5
2007	13.0
2008	13.1

ISD Scotland,
"Sexual Health: Abortions,"
May 26, 2009. www.isdscotland.org.

Abortion Is Not a Solution

Peter Kearney, spokesman for the Catholic Church in Scotland, said: "These are appalling and distressing statistics. If anything it indicates that the government's sexual health strategy, which was created by the last administration and perpetuated by the current administration, is working perfectly— because part of that strategy was fast and instant access to widespread abortion services. Unfortunately, it is completely the wrong strategy.

"Until politicians and health professionals stop counting abortion as a solution and realise what an appalling problem it is, these numbers will probably get worse.

"They are all girls below the age of consent and that asks a very serious question of GPs [doctors] in Scotland.

"To what extent did they follow this up and make sure cases were referred to the relevant authorities? Each of these cases represents a potential crime."

"Until politicians and health professionals stop counting abortion as a solution and realize what an appalling problem it is, these numbers will probably get worse."

He called for the statistics to be made freely available every year.

All Scottish schools are expected to provide sex education. Under guidelines introduced in 2001, pupils are taught that saying no to sex until they reach 16 and are in a strong and stable relationship is a "positive choice."

Youngsters are also told that stable family life is important for bringing up kids.

At the same time, they are also given information on contraception and sexual health services. The strategy is known as "abstinence-plus" and is designed to delay sexual activity among teenagers.

Kids in the early years of primary school are not given sex education but are introduced to the issue of relationships.

The government set a target to cut pregnancy rates among 13–15-year-old girls from 8.5 per 1,000—the level in 1995—to 6.8 by next year [2010]. However, they are unlikely to achieve that 20 per cent cut on current trends.

The rate varies widely around Scotland.

In Dundee, the pregnancy rate among under-16s is over 12 per 1,000. It is more [than] double the rate in Highland.

Labour health spokeswoman Cathy Jamieson said: "It is very worrying that so many young people find themselves in that position. It suggests the Scottish government needs to look again at what's in place to ensure young people get appropriate education to ensure this does not happen."

Tory health spokeswoman Mary Scanlon said: "The rising number of abortions amongst teenage girls is a serious cause of concern. We need greater education and awareness."

A Scottish government spokesman said: "We believe it is essential that young people have access to appropriate services and information about sex and relationships so that they can make informed, responsible, safe and healthy choices about their lives and relationships.

"That's why we have asked NHS boards and local authorities to ensure sexual health drop-in services for young people are available either within or near every school in Scotland."

In England, Peer-Led Sex Education Does Not Reduce Abortions

David A. Ross

David A. Ross is professor of Epidemiology & International Public Health at the London School of Hygiene & Tropical Medicine. In the following viewpoint, he reports on a study of peer-led sex education in England, in which students instructed each other. According to Ross, the study found that peer-led sex education was not any more effective than teacher-led sex education in reducing abortion and teen pregnancy. Since teacher-led sex education is usually less time-consuming and controversial, Ross suggests it may not be worth organizing peer-led programs.

As you read, consider the following questions:

1. How old were the peer teachers and students in the peer-led sexual education classes studied in the trial, according to Ross?

2. According to Ross, why might schools have been unwilling to participate in the peer-led sex education trials?

3. According to Ross, did studies in Scotland with more intensive sex education result in any difference in outcome from trials with less intensive sex education?

David A. Ross, "Approaches to Sex Education: Peer-Led or Teacher-Led?" *PLoS Medicine*, vol. 5, no. 11, November 25, 2008. Reproduced by permission.

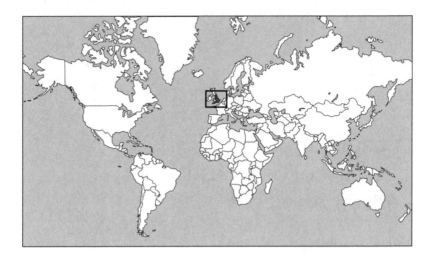

Prevention of early, unintended pregnancy, abortions, and
sexually transmitted infections among adolescents is a
very high priority in the United States and Europe, and the
United Kingdom has a target to halve pregnancy rates among
under-18-year-olds by 2010. School-based sexual health education provides an obvious approach, but evaluations of the
effectiveness of such interventions, both within high-income
and low-income countries have not been very encouraging. In
this week's [November 2008] *PLoS Medicine*, Judith Stephen-
son and colleagues report the long-term results of the . . . trial
comparing peer-led [taught by students themselves] and
teacher-led approaches, which builds on previous studies of
school-based sex education.

Peer-Led Results

Most studies to date have depended upon self-reported behav-
ioural outcomes such as pregnancy or abortion. Yet, self-
reported sexual behaviour is notoriously prone to reporting
errors, and there is considerable potential for biased misre-
porting after an intervention that aims to change behaviours.

Also, most of these previous evaluations have only had relatively short follow-up, and many have used non-randomised designs.

Despite the relatively weak evidence of the effectiveness of sexual health education as a whole, except to improve knowledge, such education is widely implemented. This is justifiable on the grounds that providing young people with the knowledge and skills to improve their sexual health can be seen as a human right and because strong evidence suggests sexual education does not encourage increased sexual activity or sexual risk.

The peer-led programme was more popular with students and the nature of the interaction in the peer-led sessions was different from the teacher-led sessions.

However, there is considerable dispute as to what the best strategy should be for sexual health education in school, with strong advocates for peer-led over the more standard teacher-led sex education.

The long-term evaluation of the effectiveness of peer-led sex education programmes in comparison with standard teacher-led sex education, . . . is therefore an important addition. Twenty-seven secondary schools in England were randomly allocated to one of two groups: One group had older (16- to 17-year-old) peers lead three one-hour classes on topics such as sexual communication, condom use, contraception, and local sexual health services for 13- to 14-year-olds in their own school. The other group received the same number of sexual education classes, but these were, as previously, led by teachers. The study showed that the peer-led programme was more popular with students and the nature of the interaction in the peer-led sessions was different from the teacher-led sessions.

In a previous report the . . . researchers showed that at age 16, girls in the peer-led group reported fewer unintended pregnancies, although this difference was of borderline statistical significance (2.3% versus 3.3%). . . . In this week's *PLoS Medicine*, the researchers report the long-term results, with follow-up to age 20 years. Such long-term follow-up makes this study unique and important. But perhaps even more significantly, the researchers did not rely only upon self-reported data on pregnancies and abortions. They also identified all pregnancies and abortions among girls that were registered in routinely reported health service data through data linkage at the individual level. This is a major strength of the trial.

The results of the trial are, however, somewhat inconclusive. In terms of abortions, although there were fewer abortions reported by girls in the peer-education arm . . . this difference was not seen in the more objective outcome data on registered abortions from the data linkage study, either up to 18 years of age . . . or up to 20 years of age. In terms of pregnancies, although fewer pregnancies were self-reported by girls in the peer-education group . . . the difference—though in the same direction—was not statistically significant in the analysis of the more objective data on registered live births either by 18.5 years of age . . . or by 20.5 years of age.

Peer-Led Is Not Better

Despite the rather inconclusive findings, the long-term results of the . . . trial are very important. First, they confirm the importance of including objective, biological outcomes in such trials, rather than only relying on self-reported data even of such salient events as pregnancy or abortion. Second, they give advocates of peer-led over teacher-led sex education reason to pause for thought. The peer-educator approach is far more labour intensive, requiring new cohorts of peer educators to be trained every year or two, and is often seen as more threatening than teacher-led sex education by school authori-

Sex Education Made Compulsory in All Schools

Sex education is to be made a compulsory part of the national curriculum [in Britain] in primary and secondary schools under government plans to cut teen pregnancies and sexually transmitted diseases.

A new . . . curriculum, expected by 2010, will include compulsory sex and relationships education as well as better advice warning children against drugs and alcohol.

Children will learn about body parts and the fact that animals reproduce from the age of five, puberty and intercourse from the age of seven and contraception and abortion from the age of 11.

Polly Curtis,
"Sex Education Made Compulsory in All Schools,"
Guardian, *October 23, 2008. www.guardian.co.uk.*

ties. This might partly explain the very low uptake of schools participating in the trial, with less than 10% of eligible schools who were invited willing to participate, though apathy and the additional work related to the evaluation may also have been factors. Although the peer-led programmes were more popular with students, the borderline evidence of greater effectiveness in this trial should make education authorities think twice before replacing teacher-led sex education with peer-led, given the important financial and logistical barriers to large-scale adoption of peer-led sex education in schools.

Furthermore, there are many unanswered questions. Both the peer-led and the teacher-led sex education programmes were fairly minimal, at only three one-hour sessions. However, . . . [a] trial in Scotland, which compared standard teacher-led sex education (seven to 12 sessions in total, largely devoted to provision of information and discussion) with a more intensive, specially designed teacher-led intervention (20 sessions in total across years three and four of secondary school [ages 13–15 years], with a focus on active learning and skills development), also found no impact on either reported or routinely registered pregnancy or abortion rates. And perhaps such in-school interventions may need to be combined with interventions to change wider norms within society, including among parents.

The peer-educator approach is far more labour intensive ... and is often seen as more threatening than teacher-led sex education by school authorities.

Despite the inconclusive results of the ... trial, the scale and importance of immediate, short-term sexual and reproductive health problems among adolescents—and the potential for sex education during adolescence to influence adoption of norms and behaviours that could reap benefits throughout their subsequent adult lives—means that we do not have the luxury of leaving things be. We must continue to develop and rigorously evaluate new approaches to reduce the adoption of sexual risk behaviours by young people. This is vital both in high-income countries such as the United Kingdom, and, even more importantly, in low-income countries, especially those with high maternal and infant mortality and incidence of HIV.

In the United States, Sex Education Contributes to High Abortion Rates

Alabama Physicians for Life

Alabama Physicians for Life sponsors PhysiciansForLife.org, a Web site devoted to drawing attention to issues such as abortion, stem cell research, and the virtues of sexual abstinence. In the following viewpoint, the organization argues that traditional sex education in the United States has encouraged a values-free approach to sex. It also contends that sex education has promoted birth control methods that are often ineffective. The only real way to prevent abortion, the organization insists, is by teaching young people to abstain from sex.

As you read, consider the following questions:

1. According to the viewpoint, who was Margaret Sanger?
2. What is the likely result of teens engaging in mutual masturbation, according to the organization?
3. According to the viewpoint, in 1991 what percentage of unplanned pregnancies did Planned Parenthood say were due to a failure of birth control?

As we begin our walk into the third millennium, we are constantly met with the present problems of teen/young adult nonmarital pregnancy, STDs [sexually transmitted dis-

Alabama Physicians for Life, "Abstinence, Sex Education & Abortion: The Connection," PhysiciansForLife.org, 2004. Copyright © 2004 PhysiciansForLife.org. All Rights Reserved. Reproduced by permission.

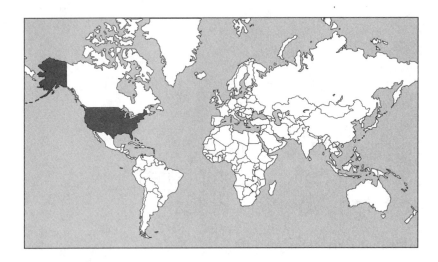

eases], emotional brokenness, suicide, failure to bond, failure to thrive, pornography, sex abuse, divorce; the list goes on. These are not technically "problems"; rather, they are all symptoms of a basic underlying problem: nonmarital sexual activity.

We have been putting generic, cheap bandages on a moribund wound. It's time to dig into the wound, find the source of infection, and thoroughly clean it out.

The Problem with Sex Ed

For the past 30–40 years, sex educators have been teaching sex education to our children under two major assumptions:

1. information will change behavior
2. teens *WILL* have sex because they cannot control themselves

These "traditional" sex educators believe that the more graphic, the more sexually detailed information given to teens is, the more "careful" they will be. That is, they believe that sexually explicit information will lead to birth control use, which will reduce teen pregnancy rates and STD infection rates because the sexual acts would have occurred anyway in "unprotected sex."

In the eyes of major sex educators such as Planned Parenthood [PP], Advocates for Youth, and SIECUS [Sexuality Information and Education Council of the United States], preventing teen pregnancy is paramount. Teens should not be discouraged from having sex; they should learn to do it "responsibly."

These "traditional" sex educators believe that the more graphic, the more sexually detailed information given to teens is, the more "careful" they will be.

As the foremost agencies of social change, SIECUS, PP and AGI (Alan Guttmacher Institute) are concerned about lowering the number of teen births. Abortion is considered a follow-up birth control, and all decisions are equal as long as the thought process is the same.

Soon after the 1973 *Roe v. Wade* decision (which legalized abortion on demand in this nation) by the U.S. Supreme Court (7–2 decision), [Planned Parenthood's] Alan Guttmacher revealed one of the primary purposes of values-free sex education when he admitted: "The only avenue the IPPF [International Planned Parenthood Federation] and its allies could travel to win the battle for abortion on demand is through sex education."

Instead of teaching youth to learn delayed gratification, self-control, and prevention through risk elimination, they have been teaching "risk reduction." Our children have been raised on risky education rather than on healthy education. They have learned all about safe and safer sex rather than about *saved sex*. The sex educators sacrificed morality for safety, but have not achieved either.

The Agenda of Sex Education

In order to understand the underlying philosophy of this "traditional" sex education, it is necessary to review some history.

Planned Parenthood of America originated from Margaret Sanger, a free thinker born in 1879, who greatly admired [Nazi leader Adolf] Hitler and his plan of eugenics [improvement of the race through controlled mating]. She "plunged" into radical politics, feminism, and permissive sex in college. Her first publication, *The Woman Rebel*, a paper of militant thought, violated the Comstock obscenity laws [created by the Comstock Act, which is named for its chief proponent Anthony Comstock], and so she fled to England to avoid prosecution. There she was influenced by Thomas Malthus, who proposed that populations grow exponentially while production grows arithmetically. Sanger began to promote birth control and abortion based on the Malthusian theory. She returned to America, was able to get the charges dropped, and formed the [American] Birth Control League which, by 1922, was privately funded and well established.

Sanger's marriage failed; she experimented extensively sexually, and finally married into wealth. She used this wealth to fight for social planning through reproductive control in various state programs.

And what is this path? It appears to be a commitment to undermine the moral value of teens.

In 1942, the Birth Control League was renamed Planned Parenthood Federation of America [PPFA] "because it had a more positive ring and conveyed a clean wholesome family-oriented image." The Alan Guttmacher Institute (AGI) is the research arm of Planned Parenthood and is named after Planned Parenthood's second president. Faye Wattleton, who replaced Guttmacher as president once said, "We are merely walking down the path Mrs. Sanger carved out for us."

And what is this path? It appears to be a commitment to undermine the moral value of teens. Wattleton also said, "We are not going to be an organization promoting celibacy and chastity."

Planned Parenthood (PP) teaches "outercourse," which means every type of sexual activity except intercourse. PP even considers outercourse a form of abstinence. PP endorses premarital sex and sexual experimentation, and considers homosexuality and heterosexuality equally acceptable lifestyles.

In the PP brochure *Sex ... The First Time or Anytime!* the young reader is informed: "Intercourse isn't the only way. Kissing, hugging, touching, masturbating, [and] oral sex, are often very exciting and satisfying."

PP has been instrumental in blocking or injuncting parental notification and consent laws (regarding minors' abortions) and informed consent laws (providing 24 hours and medical information to women considering abortion) throughout the nation over the years. PP fights fiercely against sexual abstinence programs for teens, and against decent burial or cremation for aborted babies. They also vehemently oppose health rules and regulations for abortion centers. This certainly seems to show a pattern to which most parents in this nation would object.

For example, on the issue of abstinence, most American parents want their teens to learn how and why to abstain from sexual activity outside marriage. And certainly, if they were truly concerned about women's health, they would support abortion center regulations, just as we all support health regulations for restaurants.

SIECUS and Kinsey

SIECUS is an acronym for Sexuality Information and Education Council of the United States. SIECUS was founded in 1964, has under 3,000 members, a staff of 15, and an annual budget of about $1 million. Its mission is to ensure that all people—including adolescents—have the right to affirm their sexuality as a natural part of their lives. This may sound wonderful, until one comes to understand that they work to promote the right of any individual at any age to make their own "responsible" sexual choices [i.e., use of condoms and chemical birth control]. There is a push to lower the age of sexual consent worldwide to 10 years; homosexuality and heterosexuality are to be equated.

SIECUS sees this agenda being accomplished through comprehensive sex education. Quoting SIECUS: "Homosexual, heterosexual, and bisexual are morally neutral. Incest between adults and younger children can prove to be a satisfying and enriching experience." Their position on abstinence is that it is "a good choice, but only one choice."

Debra Heffner, past president of SIECUS and Planned Parenthood educator in a training session for teacher trainers and educators, noted: "We should teach teens about oral sex and mutual masturbation in order to help them delay the onset of sexual intercourse and its resulting consequences." How many *adults* could realistically be involved in these activities and not have intercourse? Yet, she believes that teens would have that kind of control. Since she believes that, why can't she understand that teens *would have the control to abstain* by avoiding sexual activity altogether?

Amazingly, in this age of high teen pregnancy rates and STD epidemics, SIECUS writes: "Fear-based abstinence programs exaggerate the negative consequences of premarital sex." Explaining to teens the actual physical/psychological effects—the medical consequences—of "risk reduction" sexual activity is not fear-based; it shows real concern for their lives, and sincere respect for who they are as human beings.

Another actor in this movement was Alfred C. Kinsey. His works, *Sexual Behavior in the Human Male* (1948) and *Sexual Behavior in the Human Female* (1953) were "the stellar authority behind" the Model Penal Code, which was drafted in 1955 by the American Law Institute (ALI), which "deconstructed the family and paved the way for 'nontraditional families.'" Kinsey's so-called "scientific" studies were "cited and referenced by the U.S. Supreme Court when handing down the *Roe v. Wade* decision that legalized abortion in 1973."

Explaining to teens the actual physical/psychological effects . . . of "risk reduction" sexual activity is not fear-based; it shows real concern for their lives.

However, "Kinsey used unscientific fraudulent and even criminal methods in his research. He collected data from co-workers who sexually abused hundreds of minors and children as young as two months old to prove that children are sexual beings from birth and can enjoy sex with an adult. Some of his victims were subjected to more than 24 hours of nonstop sexual atrocities. Their cries of trauma and sobbing were misreported. Kinsey gathered his data using prison inmates, predatory pedophiles, and even a WWII [World War II] Nazi officer whose victims (mostly children) were forced to choose between rape or the gas chamber.

"Two videos, *The Children of Table 34* from Family Research Council and *Secret History[: Kinsey's Paedophiles]*, a BBC documentary produced in 1998, as well as books authored by Judith Reisman, Ph.D. who has extensively researched Kinsey, expose his criminal methods, false data, and entire hoax."

The ALI upheld many of Kinsey's false claims, such as "the claim that 10 percent of the population is homosexual, and that under the current state penal laws 95 percent of American males would be classified as sex offenders. ALI thus recommended the decriminalization of laws on sexual offenses such as sodomy." We have seen this come to pass with the U.S. Supreme Court decision that struck down sodomy laws.

Then, in 1954, "Kinsey collaborated with Mary S. Calderone, M.D." who "was the first medical director for Planned Parenthood and also the founder of SIECUS." Together they laid "the 'scientific' groundwork for legalizing abortion." . . .

Disastrous Results

Many teachers and administrators in public schools do not understand the mentality which Comprehensive Sex Education is pushing on our children—valueless, immediate gratification, and sexual stimulation of any kind at any time by anyone at any age for an addictive high.

Most teachers and administrators still want to support abstinence; but they have not communicated with parents. If they would, they'd find that most parents want character-based abstinence-only education, too!

Most educators and parents struggle with great concern and confusion over those students who are already sexually active. They ask, "What about the students who are going to have sex anyway?" The answer is that *ALL* students benefit from learning healthy choices; we never serve teens well by enabling their unhealthy choices. We also endanger abstaining teens when birth control methodology is discussed in the classroom because they perceive that adults want them to be sexually active.

We also endanger abstaining teens when birth control methodology is discussed in the classroom because they perceive that adults want them to be sexually active.

Birth control methods never protect the heart, and they are quite ineffective against most STDs. After 30 years of Comprehensive Sex Education, the research is clear: Condom distribution and methodology have increased sexual activity among teens in almost every study, have not lowered teen pregnancy in any study, and have not lowered overall STD problems.

Teaching teens how to use condoms for 30 years has made the situation much worse and has done nothing to promote personal responsibility, self-control, self-discipline, and other character traits such as honesty, trust, integrity, respect for others and respect for oneself. Many of our teens do not understand these traditional standards because they have been raised in a moral vacuum.

Aristotle, a pagan, wrote that for a civilization to survive and prosper, it must be based upon standards or principles called the "classical virtues": prudence, temperance, justice, and fortitude. To teach these virtues of prudence, temperance, fortitude and justice to our teens is not teaching a particular religious dogma; we will be teaching them how to help our civilization survive!

We have been frozen for years by our fear of "imposing our morality" on others. But what has happened? As we good people did nothing, evil triumphed and others "imposed their immorality" on our children.

An anonymous sage wrote: "When wealth is lost, nothing is lost; when health is lost, something is lost; when character is lost, all is lost."

If we want our civilization to survive and improve, we must break out of our fearful omissions and take action now.

A wise person once said: "You only *really* believe that which motivates you to action." Do we really believe we can help our teens to live healthy lives? Do we really believe one person can make a difference?

Solutions

First of all, we have to understand the culpability and failure of birth control. Birth control has led to infidelity in marriage, sexual experimentation, and promiscuity. Following in this wake have surfaced STD epidemics, out-of-wedlock pregnancies, sex abuse, pornography, divorce, and so on.

As regards sexually transmitted disease, it is important to note that chemical birth control methods provide NO protection against STDs/STIs [sexually transmitted infections]. If barrier and chemical birth control methods fail so much of the time to stop pregnancy *how* can we expect them to stop

Inaccurate Statistics in Abstinence Education

Each of these assertions turns up in . . . abstinence-only sex education programs: Condoms fail to prevent HIV infection 31 percent of the time. . . . The chances of getting pregnant while using a condom are 1 in 6. And condoms break or slip off nearly 15 percent of the time.

Each of them is wrong, says John Santelli, a pediatrician and [public health] professor.

Christopher Lee,
"Inaccurate Statistics Cited In Abstinence-Only Education,"
Seattle Times, *April 29, 2007. http://seattletimes.nwsource.com.*

sexually transmitted diseases, which are so much smaller than a sperm, which can be transmitted any day of the year, and many of which can be passed by skin-to-skin contact (not through fluids)?

If we know that birth control methods allow for such high failure rates, *why do we continue to promote such risky behavior*—sexual Russian Roulette—*to our young people?*

Birth control has led to infidelity in marriage, sexual experimentation, and promiscuity.

When birth control "fails" (i.e., the woman gets pregnant), abortion is pushed as "back-up birth control." Yet, in a *Wall Street Journal* letter to the editor in 1991, the International Planned Parenthood Federation (IPPF) U.S. Medical Director Dr. Louise Tyrer, made public the fact that *two-thirds* (2/3) of unplanned pregnancies are due to the failure of birth control. That is about 67%! These women are statistically much more likely to have abortions than those who were not using birth control when they unexpectedly became pregnant.

The Centers for Disease Control and Prevention (CDC) also has noted that a study conducted in 1994–95 found that 57.5% of the women procuring abortions had been using birth control methods the month they became pregnant [32.9% of the women in this study were 20–24; 45.6% were over age 24].

Similarly, researchers recently found that two-thirds (about 67%) of France's unplanned pregnancies were among women using contraceptives. A fifth of the unplanned pregnancies happened when women were on the Pill [birth control] and a tenth were among those using the intrauterine device (IUD).

In other words, the birth control methods may "fail" to stop pregnancy the majority of the time.

The IPPF official 1993 publication *Progress Postponed: Abortion in Europe in the 1990s* contains proceedings of a 1990 conference cosponsored by IPPF. The purpose of the conference was to discuss ways to "reduce abortion" through better family planning.

However, many of the speakers concluded that abortion is inseparable from contraception and is even preferable to it. Deborah Rogow of International Women's Health Coalition noted that "many abortion clients are themselves contraceptive users. . . . Despite their differences, abortion and contraception are two ways of accomplishing the same primary goal: control over one's reproduction."

At a 1995 PPFA conference, Dr. A. Kinsey stated, "At the risk of being repetitious, I would remind the group that we have found the highest frequency of induced abortion in the group which, in general, most frequently uses contraceptives."

Not only do birth control methods "fail" to stop pregnancy; the comprehensive sex educators and abortion providers have known this for many years. . . .

Secondly, from a pro-life point of view, we know that 80%–85% of all U.S. abortions are procured by unmarried girls and women. Thus, abstinence will stop the vast majority of abortions in this nation.

If we are going to stop abortion, we must each redirect at least some of our pro-life energy to preventive strategies. As Ben Franklin said, "An ounce of prevention is worth a pound of cure." By helping our young people to maintain and renew their virginity, they will avoid the heavy emotional, physical, and financial burdens.

Thirdly, we can teach sexual abstinence and chastity as a lifestyle, *not* as a birth control method. Abstinence ought to be taught as part of character education. Our training can be directive, not values neutral. Training can be designed to show the real consequences of sexual involvement with no mixed messages.

Abstinence will stop the vast majority of abortions in this nation.

Our children also need to understand that sex is an expression of love and that love is based on commitment, responsibility, trust, and respect. The only things we can mix in our education program are abstinence and character education.

As a fourth step, we can and must *involve and welcome parents* in the training process. By helping parents to develop the confidence they need to communicate with their teens, we will help to strengthen family ties.

Finally, we can understand the key position that the basic family unit holds and the importance of raising our children through an appreciation of character-based abstinence education. The basic family unit must be upheld and protected.

Whether we send our children to public, private, or home school, we must make time to teach them the basis of human relationships—respect for each other and for oneself. We can completely avoid fears and concerns of "imposing religious morality" on our teens by simply describing to them the physical and emotional consequences of uncommitted sexual activity.

It doesn't take a National Merit [Scholarship] finalist to realize that the negative consequences of uncommitted sexual activity far outweigh the momentary benefits.

If we ever hope to win the abortion battle, we must stop the cause of abortion: sexual activity outside marriage. The abortion industry has had to prey on younger and younger girls by encouraging their sexual activity in order to keep that wealthy industry going. As we teach all our adolescents the benefits of sexual abstinence and the refusal skills they need, the numbers of panicked pregnant teens will dwindle, and the abortion sites will close their doors for good. Abstinence Stops Abortion. . . .

Periodical Bibliography

The following articles have been selected to supplement the diverse views presented in this chapter.

Abortion Review	"Sex Education Not Enough, Say Researchers," November 23, 2006. www.abortionreview.org.
Alex Colman	"Two Abortions at 19: Time for Sex Education Reforms?" *Linc*, November 11, 2009. www.thelinc.co.uk.
Bruce Crumley	"U.S. Conservatives Attack UNESCO's Sex-Ed Guidelines," *Time*, September 3, 2009. www.time.com.
Linda DeLaine	"Sex and the Future of Russian Society," *Russian Life*, March 15, 2007. www.russianlife.com.
IRIN	"Kenya: Back-Street Abortions Underline Need for Sex Education," October 19, 2009. www.plusnews.org.
Suvendrini Kakuchi	"Japan: Experts Put New Spin on Sex Education," IPS, May 27, 2004. http://ipsnews.net.
Mark McDonald	"Abortions Surge in China; Officials Cite Poor Sex Education," *New York Times*, July 30, 2009. www.nytimes.com.
Graeme Paton	"Parents Lose Right over Sex Education," *Telegraph*, November 5, 2009. www.telgraph.co.uk.
Danilo Valladares	"Guatemala: Sex Education, Family Planning Finally Available," IPS, November 26, 2009. http://ipsnews.net.
Hilary White	"Thousands of Under-Age Abortions in Scotland Under Government Sex-Ed Push," LifeSiteNews.com, August 17, 2009. www.lifesitenews.com.

For Further Discussion

Chapter 1: Abortion and Religion

1. Based on your readings, do Buddhism, Hinduism, Islam, and/or Judaism oppose abortion in all circumstances? If they do ban all abortions, what are the grounds for the universal ban? If they do not, under what circumstances would they allow abortion?

2. Do Jon O'Brien and Sara Morello argue that abortion may be moral? Explain the key points in their reasoning.

Chapter 2: Abortion and the Law

1. Both William Binchy and Richard Ho Lung argue that outside forces are trying to legalize abortion in their nations. What institutions or regions do Binchy and Ho Lung blame in particular? How are their particular accusations similar and how are they different?

2. Gisela Wurm argues that abortions should not be outlawed, in part because outlawing abortion does not actually reduce the number of abortions. Are there reasons to outlaw a practice besides preventing it? In his viewpoint, what does Paul Dobbyn suggest are some reasons to keep Queensland's largely symbolic anti-abortion law? Do you find his arguments convincing?

Chapter 3: Abortion and Sex Selection

1. Based on his arguments, do you think David Heyd would approve of using abortion to terminate a fetus with Down syndrome? Would Bart Engelen and Antoon Vandevelde?

2. Joan Delaney argues that a shortage of women worldwide may lead to "widespread social unrest." What evidence does she provide for this position? Is her evidence con-

vincing—that is, do the problems she documents seem to qualify, or seem likely to lead to "widespread social unrest"? Explain your reasoning.

Chapter 4: Abortion and Sex Education

1. Many young girls in Scotland have abortions, according to the viewpoint by Magnus Gardham. How would Chloe Arnold suggest solving this problem? How would Alabama Physicians for Life suggest solving this problem? Which arguments seem more credible given the particular situation in Scotland?

2. The kinds of educational programs advocated by Chelsea Morroni and her colleagues for South Africa and IRIN for Zimbabwe are quite different. How do the programs differ, and why do these differences make sense given the legal climates in South Africa and Zimbabwe?

Organizations to Contact

The editors have compiled the following list of organizations concerned with the issues debated in this book. The descriptions are derived from materials provided by the organizations. All have publications or information available for interested readers. The list was compiled on the date of publication of the present volume; the information provided here may change. Be aware that many organizations take several weeks or longer to respond to inquiries, so allow as much time as possible.

Australian Family Association (AFA)

35 Whitehorse Road, PO Box 251, Balwyn, Victoria   3103
  Australia
03 9816 0800
Web site: www.family.org.au

The Australian Family Association (AFA) is an organization devoted to defending the family. It disseminates information about and promotes research on the family as well as advocates for policies that it identifies as family friendly. It publishes *AFA Journal,* which is distributed three times a year to AFA members, and the journal *Family Update,* which is distributed every other month.

Family Planning Association (FPA)

50 Featherstone Street, London   EC1Y 8QU
  England
020 7608 5240 • fax: 0845 123 2349
e-mail: general@fpa.org.uk
Web site: www.fpa.org.uk

Family Planning Association (FPA) is the United Kingdom's leading sexual health charity. Its purpose is to enable people in the United Kingdom to make informed choices about sex and to enjoy sexual health. FPA advocates for the right to reproductive services, disseminates information, and maintains a help line. Many publications are available on or through its Web site, including *In Brief*, a quarterly update for professional family planning providers, and *Sex Talk*, a quarterly newsletter for members.

Guttmacher Institute
125 Maiden Lane, 7th Floor, New York, NY 10038
(212) 248-1111 • fax: (212) 248-1951
e-mail: info@guttmacher.org
Web site: www.guttmacher.org

The Guttmacher Institute is a sexual and reproductive health research group. It uses statistical data and research to protect and expand the reproductive choices for men and women, including birth control and safe and legal abortion. Its publications include *Perspectives on Sexual and Reproductive Health* and *International Perspectives on Sexual and Reproductive Health*.

Human Life International (HLI)
4 Family Life Lane, Front Royal, VA 22630
(800) 549-5433 • fax: (540) 622-6247
e-mail: hli@hli.org
Web site: www.hli.org

Human Life International (HLI) is a Catholic organization working worldwide to oppose what it considers the culture of death, including abortion, contraception, and euthanasia. It lobbies lawmakers, opposes pro-choice organizations, and works with pro-life advocates internationally. Publications available on its Web site include *The Case Against Condoms* and the Pro-Life Talking Points series, which is designed to provide pro-life activists with clear and concise information.

International Consortium for Medical Abortion (ICMA)
Reproductive Health Training Center, Chisinau MD 2001
  Moldova
+373 22 54-56-09 • fax: +373 22 27-33-39

Web site: www.medicalabortionconsortium.org

The International Consortium for Medical Abortion (ICMA) brings together abortion advocates, service providers, policy makers, and researchers from all over the world to produce and disseminate information on medical abortion. It is focused on the needs of women in developing countries and in countries where abortion is unsafe or inaccessible. Its Web site includes *The ICMA Information Package on Medical Abortion* as well as medical guides, reports on abortion laws of the world, and reports on research findings about different abortion procedures.

National Abortion Federation (NAF)

1660 L Street NW, Suite 450, Washington, DC 20036
(202) 667-5881 • fax: (202) 667-5890
e-mail: naf@prochoice.org
Web site: www.prochoice.org

The National Abortion Federation (NAF) is a forum for providers of abortion services in the United States and Canada, and for others committed to making safe, legal abortions accessible to all women. It provides standards and guidelines for abortion services, and it serves as a clearinghouse of information on abortion services. NAF publishes fact sheets and bulletins, the textbook *Management of Unintended and Abnormal Pregnancy: Comprehensive Abortion Care*, and the *Clinicians for Choice* e-newsletter.

Pro-Life Philippines Foundation, Inc.

San Lorenzo Ruiz Student Catholic School
2486 Legarda Street, Sampaloc, Manila
   Philippines
(632) 692-3794 • fax: (632) 913-6433
e-mail: life@prolife.org.ph
Web site: www.prolife.org.ph

Pro-life Philippines Foundation, Inc. is a nonprofit pro-life organization active throughout the Philippines. It works to disseminate information about the dangers of abortion and also lobbies politicians and legislators. Its Web site features reports and articles including "Abortion Has Greater Impact on Parenting" as well as discussions on the lives and teachings of pro-life saints.

United Nations Population Fund (UNFPA)
220 East Forty-second Street, New York, NY   10017
(212) 297-5000 • fax: (212) 370-0201
e-mail: hq@unfpa.org
Web site: www.unfpa.org

United Nations Population Fund (UNFPA) is an international development agency. It supports countries in using population data for policies and programs to reduce poverty and to ensure that every pregnancy is wanted, every birth is safe, every young person is free of HIV/AIDS, and every girl and woman is treated with dignity and respect. To meet these goals it distributes information and works to ensure quality medical care worldwide. Its Web site offers numerous publications and reports, including *Ensuring Access to Reproductive Health Supplies* and *Reducing Unmet Need for Family Planning.*

United States Conference of Catholic Bishops (USCCB)
3211 Fourth Street NE, Washington, DC   20017-1194
(202) 541-3000
Web site: www.usccb.org

The United States Conference of Catholic Bishops (USCCB), which adheres to the Vatican's opposition of abortion, is a coalition of American Roman Catholic bishops. While pursuing its ultimate goal of a legal ban on abortion, USCCB suggests that states restrict abortion by passing parental consent/ notification laws and strict licensing laws for abortion clinics. Its publications include the annual magazine *Respect Life* and the newsletter *Life Insight.*

World Health Organization (WHO)
Avenue Appia 20, Geneva 27   1211
   Switzerland

+41 22 791 21 11 • fax: +41 22 791 31 11
e-mail: info@who.int
Web site: www.who.int

The World Health Organization (WHO) is the United Nations specialized agency for health. Established in 1948, WHO seeks to promote the highest possible level of health for all people. Health is defined in WHO's constitution as a state of complete physical, mental, and social well-being and not merely the absence of disease or infirmity. WHO is governed by 193 member countries through the World Health Assembly. WHO's Web site contains a library of reports and publications as well as links to various world health journals and reports. Abortion-related publications include *Mid-Level Health-Care Providers Are a Safe Alternative to Doctors for First-Trimester Abortions in Developing Countries* and *Facts on Induced Abortion Worldwide*.

Bibliography of Books

Alaka Malwade Basu	*The Sociocultural and Political Aspects of Abortion: Global Perspectives.* Westport, CT: Praeger, 2003.
Jonathan E. Brockopp, ed.	*Islamic Ethics of Life: Abortion, War, and Euthanasia.* Columbia, SC: University of South Carolina, 2003.
Albin Eser and Hans-Georg Koch	*Abortion and the Law: From International Comparison to Legal Policy.* The Hague, Netherlands: TMC Asser Press, 2005.
Ann Farmer	*By Their Fruits: Eugenics, Population Control, and the Abortion Campaign.* Washington, DC: Catholic University of America Press, 2008.
Gideon Haigh	*The Racket: How Abortion Became Legal in Australia.* Carlton, Victoria: Melbourne University Press, 2008.
Gordon Horobin, ed.	*Experience with Abortion: A Case Study of North-East Scotland.* Cambridge, UK: Cambridge University Press, 2009.
Mala Htun	*Sex and the State: Abortion, Divorce, and the Family Under Latin American Dictatorships and Democracies.* Cambridge, UK: Cambridge University Press, 2003.

Masae Kato   *Women's Rights? The Politics of Eugenic Abortion in Modern Japan.* Amsterdam, Netherlands: Amsterdam University Press, 2009.

Lara M. Knudsen   *Reproductive Rights in a Global Context: South Africa, Uganda, Peru, Denmark, United States, Vietnam, Jordan.* Nashville, TN: Vanderbilt University Press, 2006.

Phillip B. Levine   *Sex and Consequences: Abortion, Public Policy, and the Economics of Fertility.* Princeton, NJ: Princeton University Press, 2004.

Daniel C. Maguire   *Sacred Rights: The Case for Contraception and Abortion in World Religions.* New York: Oxford University Press, 2003.

Marc L. Moskowitz   *The Haunting Fetus: Abortion, Sexuality, and the Spirit World in Taiwan.* Honolulu, HI: University of Hawaii Press, 2001.

Jing-Bao Nie   *Behind the Silence: Chinese Voices on Abortion.* Lanham, MD: Rowman & Littlefield Publishers, 2005.

Tiana Norgren   *Abortion Before Birth Control: The Politics of Reproduction in Postwar Japan.* Princeton, NJ: Princeton University Press, 2001.

Tulsi Patel, ed.

Sex-Selective Abortion in India: Gender, Society and New Reproductive Technologies. Thousand Oaks, CA: Sage Publications, 2007.

Daniel Schiff

Abortion in Judaism. Cambridge, UK: Cambridge University Press, 2002.

Jennifer Schweppe, ed.

The Unborn Child, Article 40.3.3 and Abortion in Ireland: Twenty-Five Years of Protection? Dublin, Ireland: Liffey Press, 2008.

Lisa Smyth

Abortion and Nation: The Politics of Reproduction in Contemporary Ireland. Burlington, VT: Ashgate Publishing Company, 2005.

Irene Vilar

Impossible Motherhood: Testimony of an Abortion Addict. New York: Other Press, 2009.

Leela Visaria and Vimala Ramachandran, eds.

Abortion in India: Ground Realities. New Delhi, India: Routledge India, 2007.

Index

Geographic headings and page numbers in **boldface** refer to viewpoints about that country or region.